Essentials for People Care and Development

MISSIO NEXUS IMPROVE SERIES

Essentials for People Care and Development

A Collection of Best Practices,
Research, Reflections, and Strategies

Geoff Whiteman and Heather Pubols, eds.

MISSIO NEXUS®

Missio Nexus, Wheaton, IL
Published 2023
Printed in the United States of America

ISBN-13: 9798861222310 (paper)

The cover was designed and interior typeset by Kurtis Amundson.

DEDICATION

To our spouses
for participating with us on all the twists
and turns of this missionary journey.

To all of our missionary friends and colleagues
persevering through numerous challenges to
be the people God created them to be.

To all the people helpers and member care professionals
laboring to fulfill the Great Commission though
keeping the greatest commandments of love.
Thank you for caring for God's beloved
missionaries and doing so with competence.

To the triune God – Father, Son, and Holy Spirit.
May this offering be received for Your Glory
and for the edification of your Body
and for the salvation of the world.

Contents

I · Engaging the Cross in Member Care

II · Engaging Our Changing World in Member Care

Foreword

We are grateful and humbled to be asked to help introduce this important volume on people care and development in the Missio Nexus Improve Series. At the same time, we are excited to review the contents from this early standpoint, and therefore very interested about where this is all going.

We have served in missions for many years and are a couple of the *chronologically-gifted* pioneers of the member care/development process. Having both authored several books and many articles on this topic – this history caused us to look at this volume by a variety of specialists ... and wish we'd had access to it years ago!

The book begins with "The Stories We Tell and Why They Matter." This topic anchors the following discussions in biblical truth. Jesus' last words were "In this world you will have tribulation" (John 16:31). Mission work is frontline work. We have an enemy, and he will do anything he can to sabotage and disrupt God's work. So, it is strategic to begin with considering the topic of suffering, and what shapes our own narratives of suffering.

The second author deals with stories of resilience and what we can learn from them. Next, you can explore reasons for attrition, a tragic and often unnecessary loss of personnel. Trauma and crisis happen in missions – always has and always will. James Covey discusses trauma informed staff care.

Celeste Allen shares about the way simple hospitality can provide just what global workers need to be refreshed on their journey. And Vernon Salter wraps up the first part with ideas to create an environment for growth – not escapism. He explains that kingdom collaboration is what care in the way of Christ looks like.

The next half of the book shifts its focus to broader issues about missionary care starting with Michele Okimura discussing women's issues and suggesting ways of strengthening and empowering these workers. Most missionaries are women, so it is encouraging and enlightening to see her chapter. Then Faith De La Cour gives a practical tool for equipping individuals and families with tools for accurate assessment and readiness.

David Dunaetz focuses on conflict – and there is conflict in missions on all levels! Another necessary issue covered in "Supervisory Relationships and Well-Being" has to do with organizational leadership and promoting an ethos of well-being through policies and practices. A skillful and widely experienced voice in legal matters, Theresa Sidebotham, alerts us to the linkage between personnel dilemmas and legal concerns. Sara and Jeff Simon then provide helpful context and useful tips on periods of withdrawal (or long and brief sabbaticals) for continued spiritual growth.

The book closes with a final chapter from Geoff Whiteman giving his treatise on the "Heart of Member Care."

We have grown accustomed to looking back over what member care has become and how it is working. There is much to be excited about, and some to be concerned about. One of the stances we took early on was to align very closely with a somewhat autonomous counseling orientation that often looked at the individual away from their community, team, and background.

It is exciting to see the contributors of this volume grapple with environmental issues, investigating organizational and leadership dynamics as *care* resources, forecasting in the realm of resilience, and understanding current arenas of trauma informed climates and care. And finally, looking at the oftentimes overlooked underlying legal issues that can become snares to good intentions.

Going forward from here, we would encourage everyone to seek to better understand the current missiological dialogues occurring in the larger missional ventures. While we are beginning to benefit from analyzing organization leadership and structure (e.g., Drage and Kim), our organizations are talking about and implementing ideas from polycentric leadership theory. How will that impact member care desires and requirements?

Another issue is the continuing dialogues around the indigenization of mission structure and activity. Both future possibilities will significantly impact who does member care, as well as how it is done. At the very least, we need to be attending broader meetings to add in member care and development perspectives.

One final thought is how Artificial Intelligence (AI) and developed content might change the ways we relate to each other, both individually and with regard to the way content is delivered to our staff. What is the fine-line between technology derived content treatments, and our spiritually empowered ability to transcend beyond to heart-felt, spiritual adjustments and solutions. Our doing and being as resource people require we do and be so within the larger picture of mission.

In conclusion, we are excited about the numerous resources and areas of ministry that are outlined in the volume. Member care and development appears to be spreading out into areas with wider influence and moving into a flourishing mindset.

Thanks so much, everyone!

LAURA MAE ("LARRIE") GARDNER, DMin, is a pioneer in member care and authored *Healthy, Resilient and Effective in Cross-Cultural Ministry* as well as hundreds of articles and chapters in books. She serves on boards, consults with mission organizations, and teaches seminars and workshops around the world. Larrie and her late husband, Dick, served more than 60 years with SIL (sil.org) and Wycliffe (wycliffe.org). She lives in Tucson, Arizona and has two sons, two daughters-in-law and 8+ grandchildren.

BRENT LINDQUIST, PhD, is a pastor/missionary with JARON Ministries International (jaron.org) and the president emeritus of the Link Care Center (linkcare.org). He leads a number of cohorts in the areas of spirituality assessment and other member care issues. He and his wife, Colleen, have been married since 1974, and have two married adult children and five grandchildren.

Preface

In March of 2010 I (Heather) sent a writer and photographer to Mozambique to gather Great Commission stories from there. They spent hours over several days interviewing and photographing people and observing their life and work. After the trip, an interviewee described the visit as "better than therapy."

A couple of years later, I and another colleague traveled to a remote city in the Democratic Republic of the Congo to gather more stories. Over two intense days, we heard amazing testimonies about God's work there. But in between our interviews, several people told us, "Your visit has reminded us that God has not forgotten us."

Since 2000, I have served missions in communications. These days much of my work is focused on equipping and encouraging other missionary communicators. I often tell them that the job of a missions communicator is more than just developing content and materials to promote a mission organization's vision and programs. As we help our missionary colleagues share their knowledge and stories, in the process, we care for them as encouragers and advocates.

World Evangelical Alliance Global Member Care Network Coordinator Harry Hoffman has a category for people giving this kind of care. He calls them "people helpers." Harry says this group includes lay counselors, mentors, peers, and *spiritual mothers* and *fathers*. I might add *colleagues* to his list. People helpers are an often untapped or overlooked source of peer-related member care.

In his book *Renovated: God, Dallas Willard and the Church that Transforms*, Jim Wilder decries the neglect of relational skills development in Christian organizations. Instead, he says, as we collectively strive to accomplish our organization's vision, staff tire, disconnect, and become spiritually dead.

However, Wilder goes on to explain that when our organizations first cultivate healthy relational cultures, vision is implemented in a better way. People stop "burning out for Jesus," mature spiritually, and exhibit greater trust in God. Member care in this model becomes a critical organizational strategy for sustainability, and *everyone* is invited to play a part in it.[1]

This brings me great encouragement and was part of my inspiration in spearheading the creation of this book. My desire was not just to see member care professionals better equipped. I also wanted anyone involved in missions to have the chance to expand their view of member care and see ways they could apply the contents of this book as they cared for their fellow humans serving in God's mission.

To achieve these objectives, I partnered with Geoff Whiteman. Geoff has served as a member care professional in private practice and with mission sending and service organizations (both as a resilience researcher and a marriage and family therapist), and currently advises member care professionals directly. Together as co-editors of this book, we bring our experience as co-laboring missionaries as well as our perspectives from different ends of the member care spectrum. Geoff gave leadership to this book's topics and authors, while I worked with each author on crafting the content for a broad audience.

So, whether you are a person who simply wants to be more aware of how to better care for global workers you know or work with, you are considering a ministry of care for God's beloved missionaries, or you are a seasoned member care professional – welcome! This book was written for you.

Most of the contributors to this volume presented at the Missio Nexus Mission Leaders Conference in 2022 and 2023. The themes of those conferences were "Counting the Cost" and "Shift: Rapid Social Transformation and the Gospel." The people

---

1 Jim Wilder, *Renovated: God, Dallas Willard, and the Church that Transforms* (Colorado Springs, CO: NavPress, 2020), 176.

care and development workshop track connected these themes with the needs of the missions community through a practical theology lens.

To develop this, we asked several questions. What do member care professionals believe (theological and biblical reflections)? What do we know (research and case studies)? How can we respond (frameworks and strategies)? What will help (tools and resources)? And who can we join (kingdom collaboration)?

An axiom of missiology is that faithfulness to the universal gospel requires attentiveness to the particulars. We need exegesis of the text and ethnography of the context if the good news is to be good news here and now. This axiom is true for member care as well. There have been seismic shifts in the world which impact missions and the discipline of member care.

I (Geoff) can think of many people who have lamented to me about what they are seeing. An executive director of a mid-sized agency explained, "We used to have a good handle on member care, but now we're not so sure. Everyone coming is carrying so much trauma. We want to help them, and we also have a job we need them to do."

A seasoned trainer told me, "We keep seeing major member care issues in our trainees. The people coming through training now need more training, but organizations are placing a lower priority on training. There's a huge gap between everyone's expectations. I've given my life to closing this gap, but it keeps widening."

On another occasion, a senior pastor shared with me about texting with global workers on the other side of the world that were in a medical emergency with their child. He said, "I'm their pastor. I have to help them, but I don't know who to turn to."

I share Heather's conviction that the invitation of member care to love one another well belongs to each of us. And I add my conviction that some of us are invited to become member care professionals who do so with excellence. This is because many of the perplexing and pervasive challenges are best understood as structural. These are places where our walls are not framed plumb and square to our foundation and where no amount of fresh paint will remedy the problem.

One of the more pervasive structural problems is the belief that the aim of member care is to eliminate preventable attrition rather than to see reductions in attrition as an outcome of a healthy system of which member care has a key role. Through research, we found that attrition is multi-faceted, complex, and rarely (if ever) clearly differentiated between preventable or unpreventable.[2] Member care workers often play an essential role in helping global workers do well, but their work is often tertiary and occurs alongside friends, family, colleagues, supporting churches, and others.

To move forward we need to grow in awareness of how care fits across cultures in individual relationships and in organizational systems. And we need to approach this area with hearts and minds that honor those who came before us and are open to the diverse perspectives of those involved in today's global mission environment. Reading and interacting with the content of this book can be one step in moving forward.

---

2 See Andrea Sears's chapter in this book on the "Top Ten Reasons for Missionary Attrition" for more information.

Using This Book

INDEPENDENT STUDY. This volume could assist your formational exploration of member care. The chapters are loosely organized around a practical theology framework. Collectively they form a textured view of how to approach this topic with fidelity to what is unchanging and eternal and fidelity to the always shifting context of the world we live in. We encourage you to dig deeper into the fundamental questions of member care, and we hope this volume will inspire you in your own participation.

SMALL GROUP STUDY. Each author has included discussion questions at the end of their chapter so this volume can be utilized in a small group context for enrichment or professional development. Consider meeting with your group once a month and working through this volume over the next year. Everyone can read the chapter, explore the additional resources, and be prepared to share.

A simple discussion framework, in addition to the existing questions, might be:

- *What?* What was the chapter about? Summarize the main points; highlight a few quotes.
- *So what?* How did this chapter resonate with your lived experience? What questions did it raise for you? Where do you see things similarly and differently from the author? Why?
- *Now what?* What action do you need to take, no matter how small, as a result of this discussion – personally and professionally? Individually and collectively?

Our prayer is that this book will meet a real need you have now, and provide you with resources you can return to again and again. We trust it proves to be a blessing to you and through you to those God invites you to care for. We hope you'll share it with someone you know and the dialogue that follows will spark new insights.

May we each be a part of building healthy relational cultures in the organizations we serve!

HEATHER PUBOLS is the editor of *Evangelical Missions Quarterly* (*EMQ*, emqonline.com) – a professional journal for North American missionaries that has been continuously published since 1964. She is also the founder and principal communications consultant for le Motif (lemotif.org) – a communications consulting firm focused on global mission. She has served in missions since 2000.

GEOFF WHITEMAN, ThM, LMFT, serves member care professionals as the director of the Valeo Research Institute (valeo.global/research) and the Missio Nexus People Care and Development track co-leader. Since 2000, he has served in vocational ministry and has supported the care and training of global workers in Christ since 2007. Those experiences piqued his interest in how global workers could persevere with joy which led him to research resilience (resilientglobalworker.org).

I · Engaging the Cross in Member Care

CHAPTER 1

The Stories We Tell and Why They Matter

By Kimberly Drage and Tim J. Davy

ARE EFFORTS TO CARE FOR GLOBAL WORKERS going too far in alleviating the necessary risk and suffering that comes with this work? Or is it possible that our acceptance of suffering in kingdom endeavors has created a tolerance for under-resourcing cross-cultural ministers?

These questions highlight the inherent tension between suffering and well-being in cross-cultural ministry. The very life of wholeness we invite others to in Christ was made possible through Christ's suffering. As ministers of the gospel, following Christ's example, we expect suffering, and, at the same time, we acknowledge the importance of actively supporting the well-being of cross-cultural workers (i.e., reducing their suffering).

The ways we choose to make meaning in the midst of this tension (and others like it) shape our attitudes, our actions, and, ultimately, our team and organizational cultures. The stories (narratives) we tell as individuals and organizations in the midst of this tension are powerful.

That is why it is imperative that those of us who care about the well-being of cross-cultural ministers continuously engage in thoughtful reflection, conversation, and prayerful discernment as

We use stories to answer our *why* questions, weaving meaning into our experiences.

we choose what stories we tell ourselves and each other as we engage suffering in global missions.

Suffering and the Biblical Text

Jason and Katya had been missionaries in the Middle East for 9 years when the day they had dreaded since before they ever moved finally came. There, in the customs hallway, Jason, Katya and their three children were pulled aside to a separate room where they were informed that their entry had been denied and they would need to return to their passport country. As the implications of the situation began to settle in, they wondered: *What went wrong? What will we do now? Why is this happening?*

We use stories to answer our *why* questions, weaving meaning into our experiences. These narratives can also be seen as lenses. Just as changing our glasses will change the way we see, our choice of narrative will emphasize some aspects of a situation, downplay others, and ignore still others. These explanatory narratives influence not only how a person and those around them describe and understand their experience of hardship, but also how they relate and respond to it. This certainly has implications for one's well-being.[1]

The Bible's diverse narratives of suffering offer multiple ways

---

1 Drawing on, for example, the work of Lakoff and Johnson, 2003, who talk about metaphors highlighting, downplaying, and hiding aspects of that which they are describing; for example, chapters 3 and 22. George Lakoff, and Mark Johnson, *Metaphors We Live By* (Chicago: Chicago University Press, 2003).

NARRATIVES OF SUFFERING IN THE BIBLE

PERSECUTION LENS	SPIRITUAL WARFARE LENS	DISCIPLINE LENS	COST LENS	SIN LENS	MYSTERY LENS
SUFFERING IS THE RESULT OF HOSTILITY TOWARD THE PEOPLE OF GOD BECAUSE OF WHO THEY ARE.	SUFFERING IS INITIATED BY SPIRITUAL FORCES.	SUFFERING IS A FORM OF DISCIPLINE, DESIGNED BY GOD TO FORM OUR CHARACTER.	SUFFERING IS PART OF THE COSTLY NATURE OF FOLLOWING JESUS.	SUFFERING IS THE CONSEQUENCE OF SIN.	SUFFERING, AT TIMES, HAS NO EXPLANATION.

to view these experiences. This can help us powerfully shape both our understanding of and our responses to suffering. It can also keep us from the temptation to lump suffering into one catch-all category, and opens us to the possibility that the causes of suffering may not be clear.[2]

PERSECUTION LENS. Throughout the biblical story the people of God have faced opposition from a world that is hostile to the people of God because of who they are. Biblical examples of persecution include the harsh treatment of the Hebrew people enslaved in Egypt, the threat to the nation in the story of Esther, the systematic attempts to destroy the early church in Acts, or the vitriolic attacks on believers featured in the book of Revelation.

SPIRITUAL WARFARE LENS. Attacks on believers are not solely the preserve of human beings. Paul declares in Ephesians 6:12 that

---

2 See Imamura, 2019, for a complementary list. Yuzo Imamura, "Suffering and Mission: Narrative Research from Cambodia," in *Tackling Trauma: Global, Biblical and Pastoral Perspectives*, ed. Paul A. Barker, (Carlisle, Cumbria: Langham Global Library, 2019).

Christians are wrestling against spiritual forces at work in the heavenly places. Similarly, Daniel and the book of Revelation offer us glimpses behind the curtain to describe spiritual warfare. Peter warns his readers to be watchful for the schemes of the devil, who "prowls around like a roaring lion, seeking someone to devour" (1 Peter 5:8).

DISCIPLINE LENS. In contrast to unwelcoming suffering, some hardship is interpreted in the Bible as being a form of discipline, designed by God to form our character as a loving act of parenthood. This is stated in Proverbs 3:11–12 and reiterated in Hebrews 12:3–17 when the writer exhorts readers to persevere in a pressured context.

COST LENS. Hardship in the Christian life and in Christian service is sometimes understood as being part of the costly nature of following Jesus. In Luke 14:25–33, Jesus sets out the high cost of discipleship, indicating how his followers must be prepared to give up all they hold dear. The apostle Paul gives a window into the many hardships he faced, recounting in 2 Corinthians 11:16–12:10 a litany of losses and hardships he experienced in pursuit of his calling.

SIN LENS. It is evident throughout Scripture that much hardship arises as the consequence (intended or unintended) of a person's greed, selfishness, and grasping for power and status. Cain's murder of Abel, the horrific violence recounted in Judges 19, and David's abuse of power in 2 Samuel 11 exemplify some of these. The Psalter is replete with instances of the distress caused by others and the suffering meted out by the wicked (see Psalm 10 for an example).

MYSTERY LENS. Finally, there is evidence in Scripture that some suffering seems to happen without reason. The book of Job discusses such *unattributed* suffering. Although this might seem counterintuitive given its opening chapters, the book is there not to explain where suffering comes from but to help believers know how to process their suffering with honesty and faith, even (especially) when there is no obvious cause.[3]

Employing Theological Narratives in the Face of Suffering

Let's return to the example of Jason and Katya's family and use these lenses to explore the implications of our narratives.

PERSECUTION LENS. Was the refusal a deliberate targeting of them by authorities because of their faith? This lens emphasizes the idea of hostile opposition and righteous innocence on behalf of the family.

SPIRITUAL WARFARE LENS. Was the refusal a result of spiritual battle? This narrative frames the family as being in the *right* before God, and promotes the authorities as being (perhaps unwittingly) a pawn in the schemes of the evil one.

DISCIPLINE LENS. Was the refusal a means by which God is teaching the family such virtues as reliance on God and patience? This lens places a burden of understanding on the family. It also emphasizes the need not to complain but to accept the lesson.

COST LENS. Was the refusal part of the cost of ministry? If so, this lens emphasizes the need to accept that frustrations and hardships are part of the ministry to which they have been called.

---

3 Tim J. Davy, *The Book of Job and the Mission of God: A Missional Reading* (Eugene, Oregon: Pickwick, 2020). See also David J. A. Clines, *World Bible Commentary, Vol 17: Job 1–20* (Nashville, Tennessee: Thomas Nelson, 1989), xxxviii–xxxix.

Any one interpretation of the causes of an event can be used rightly or wrongly depending on the context.

SIN LENS. Was the refusal due to the greed or selfishness of the local or national decision-makers? If so, the *sin* narrative emphasizes the innocence of the family in the situation and their righteous position in the events. They become victims in the wrong decisions of others.

Was it because the family had breached a law or failed to follow through with some aspect of their paperwork? The sin lens also invites us to critically assess ourselves and acknowledge that, at times, our difficult circumstances are caused by our own unwise actions or negligent or selfish choices (though, this would not include instances of human errancy, such as forgetting or misunderstanding).

MYSTERY LENS. Was the refusal just something that *happens*? If so, the *mystery* lens emphasizes the unclear meaning behind the event. There is no discernible reason behind the decision, and therefore no firm conclusions can be made about why it has happened.

As we see from these examples, employing different theological narratives around one event can lead to profoundly different responses and potential outcomes. This is why it is important to identify the narratives we are employing in any given situation and evaluate their appropriateness. Any one interpretation of the causes of an event can be used rightly or wrongly depending on the context. Just as wearing reading glasses to drive would actually obscure rather than clarify one's vision.

Let's consider this question again: *Are efforts to care for global workers going too far in alleviating the necessary risk and suffering that comes with this work?* At first glance, "necessary risk and suffering" seems to signal the *cost narrative*. Cross-cultural ministers *should* expect hardship. Therefore, we *should not* waste resources attempting to fix what is simply part of this work.

Yet the *cost narrative* is one among many theological narratives of suffering in the Bible. If we consider other narratives as an explanation for suffering in missions, we can ask deeper questions resulting in richer engagement.[4] For example:

- In general, what types of suffering found in the biblical text do we encounter in missions? (Or how might we understand suffering in this case?)
- What types of suffering do we have the capacity to alleviate, and which are out of our control?
- What, therefore, is the purpose and role of care departments in global missions and how can we focus our efforts most effectively?

Jason and Katya's experience of suffering illustrates that broad generalizations can be unhelpful in aiding understanding. Moreover, assigning a cause for suffering that is out of alignment with the specific context can be harmful. Each situation invites us to curiosity and deeper exploration. By proceeding with humility, discernment, and a posture aimed at understanding, we are best equipped to choose the most appropriate suffering lens.

Suffering and Nonprofit HRM Literature

The stories we tell within global missions are particularly powerful because they tend to bring in God. As Christians in the workplace,

---

4 Ann L. Cunliffe, "On Becoming a Critically Reflexive Practitioner," *Journal of Management Education* 28, no. 4 (August 2004): 407–26, https://doi.org/10.1177/1052562904264440.

this is entirely appropriate. At the same time, bringing God into our stories adds a weight that has the capacity to manipulate as well as inspire. Sometimes the assumptions shaping our stories are not purely theological even though we, or our communities, have framed them that way.

Narratives from nonprofit Human Resources Management literature bear a striking resemblance to common theological narratives we adopt in mission contexts. This offers a non-theological perspective on our stories we can use to reflect on our organizational cultures.

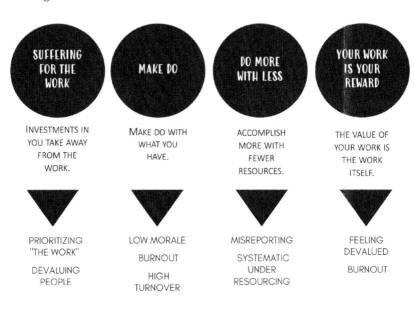

SUFFERING FOR THE WORK	MAKE DO	DO MORE WITH LESS	YOUR WORK IS YOUR REWARD
Investments in you take away from the work.	Make do with what you have.	Accomplish more with fewer resources.	The value of your work is the work itself.
▼	▼	▼	▼
Prioritizing "the work" Devaluing people	Low morale Burnout High turnover	Misreporting Systematic under resourcing	Feeling devalued Burnout

SUFFERING FOR THE WORK LENS. A common assumption in the nonprofit context is that fewer investments in administrative costs, such as staff and infrastructure, is a sign of efficiency. This narrative can normalize prioritizing *the work* over and above the people and resources needed to carry it out.[5] In some cases, this

---

5 H. L. Carpenter, "Talent Management" in *The Nonprofit Human Resource*

assumption can lead to the notion that staff *should* be suffering (low salaries, poor equipment, etc.) so the work can flourish.[6]

MAKE DO LENS. Nonprofit organizations can take on a mentality of *making do* with what they have rather than pursuing what they need. One way this happens is by putting people in roles where they are unqualified, undertrained and under-resourced.[7] The result can lead to low morale, high turnover, poor work outcomes and even burnout.[8]

DO MORE WITH LESS LENS. Monitoring the amount of money spent on overhead in nonprofit organizations has led to institutionalizing doing more with less. At times, this has resulted in under-reporting or misreporting what is actually used or needed leading to systemic under-resourcing.[9]

YOUR WORK IS YOUR REWARD LENS. A culture of under-resourcing can also be traced to the *donative labor* hypothesis – the idea that

---

Management Handbook: From Theory to Practice (New York, New York: Routledge, 2017), 122–41, https://doi.org/10.4324/9781315181585.

6 "About Fund the People," Fund the People, 2023, https://fundthepeople.org/#about.

7 Beth Gazley, "Theories of the Nonprofit Sector," in *The Nonprofit Human Resource Management Handbook: From Theory to Practice* (New York, New York: Routledge, 2017), 15–28.

8 Kennard Wing and Mark A. Hager, "Getting What We Pay For: Low Overhead Limits Nonprofit Effectiveness," *Nonprofit Overhead Cost Project*, Indiana University: Center on Philanthropy & The Urban Institute Center on Nonprofits and Philanthropy, June 4, 2016, Policy Commons, https://policycommons.net/artifacts/636109/getting-what-we-pay-for/1617415/.

9 Ann Goggins Gregory and Don Howard, "The Nonprofit Starvation Cycle," *Stanford Social Innovation Review* 7, no. 4 (2009): 49–53, https://doi.org/10.48558/6K3V-0Q70.

because the work is meaningful, people will be willing to do it for less money or with inadequate resources. Income becomes less important, and perhaps even positive feedback is not emphasized.[10] Overemphasizing the meaningfulness of the work as compensation can make employees feel unimportant and can lead to low morale and burnout, as well.[11]

Narratives influence how resources are managed and how people are viewed and treated. What do you notice as you engage these common narratives from the non-profit world?

- Have you seen cross-cultural workers experience guilt for asking for what they need? Have you observed them feeling afraid of being thought of as unspiritual? Have they expressed feeling shame for taking a vacation?
- Have you noticed a tendency for mission organizations to under-resource support structures and staff because they want to prioritize the mission? Have you detected that they are hesitant to invest in services or benefits that would help their people? Have you seen organizations face temptation to skew the communication of their needs?
- Have you ever experienced undertrained and under-resourced leaders struggling but not knowing where to reach out for help or feeling ashamed to seek help at all? Could a sense of calling lead to over-confidence when taking on a leadership role? Are there times when leadership failure is framed as personal or spiritual failure rather than a lack of training or resourcing?

How do our theological narratives align with these common

---

10 Mirae Kim and Étienne Charbonneau, "Caught Between Volunteerism and Professionalism: Support by Nonprofit Leaders for the Donative Labor Hypothesis," *Review of Public Personnel Administration* 40, no. 2 (June 1, 2020): 327–49, https://doi.org/10.1177/0734371X18816139.
11 Beth Gazley, "Theories of the Nonprofit Sector," 15–28.

Narratives influence how resources are managed and how people are viewed and treated.

lenses found in the non-profit world? Or as we asked earlier: *Is it possible that our acceptance of suffering in kingdom endeavors has created a tolerance for under-resourcing ministers?*

Tolerance for under-resourcing ministers is entirely possible. These narrative lenses from non-theological frameworks may be alive and well in our own contexts, but *dressed up* in *theological clothing*. What narratives do we want to cultivate in our organizational cultures? Acknowledging our narratives gives us the power to discern which stories we want to keep telling.

Practical Application

Let's look at narratives of suffering in your own context. Start with an event, idea or policy related to suffering in your organization or ministry (for example, the burnout of a staff member or the collapse of a ministry project).

CONSIDER WHAT NARRATIVES ARE PRESENT IN THIS SITUATION.

- Are there any connections to biblical or nonprofit narratives of suffering?
- How has this idea or policy developed? (If it is an event, how is it being approached?)
- What insights are emerging for you as you explore these questions?
- What key voices are shaping these narratives?
- What voices need to be included?

IDENTIFY THE DEEPER QUESTIONS THESE NARRATIVES RAISE.

- What makes these narratives important to you or your organization?
- What are these lenses keeping you from seeing?
- What is at the heart of these narratives?

CONSIDER THE IMPLICATIONS OF THESE NARRATIVES.

- Do they highlight anything that is unresolved in you or your organization?
- Do they open up any new possibilities?

DISCERN YOUR WAY FORWARD.

- With what do you need to spend more time?
- Who needs to be part of this conversation?
- How will this decision shape you?
- How will this shape your context?
- Who can help move this forward?
- What specific actions do you want to take?[12]

What did you notice as you engaged this process?

Engaging in Suffering Well

Tension between suffering and well-being is inherent in cross-cultural ministry. How we engage this tension matters. The stories we choose to tell ourselves and others while we suffer have the power to shape our understandings of that suffering and our responses to it.

Through the process of humbly identifying our narratives of suffering, we are invited to come together to look more deeply

---

12 Cunliffe, "On Becoming," 407–26.

at each context, listen more intently to global workers, resist easy answers, and bring the tensions we encounter before God through prayer. As we do, we draw our awareness to "what we, and others, might be taking for granted – what is being said and not said – and examining the impact this has or might have."[13]

From this place, we can begin discerning the most helpful narratives for going forward and making informed actions. This is not only a powerful way to journey with those who are suffering, but also a responsibility we steward before God.

KIMBERLY DRAGE serves Novo UK (novouk.org) in organization-member relations. As a researcher, coach and collaborator, she devotes herself to supporting the vital role of organizational health in global worker well-being. She has been ministering overseas (Asia and Europe) since 2006.

TIM DAVY is a lecturer and head of research and consultancy at All Nations Christian College in the UK (allnations.ac.uk). His PhD explored a missional reading of the book of Job. He teaches mainly in the areas of Bible and mission, and vulnerable children. He also contributes to the college's MA programme in staff care and wellbeing.

---

13 Cunliffe, "On Becoming," 741.

Questions for Reflection

- In what specific ways do you think awareness of your stories can influence your capacity to care for global workers?
- How might the concepts in this chapter be applied to situations other than suffering? What do you notice as you explore this possibility?
- What is one change you could make in your personal or organizational rhythms to attune to the narratives at play in various situations? What would happen if you did that? What values does that connect to for you?

Additional Resources

Martin-Cuellar, Ashley. "Self-Reflexivity Through Journaling: An Imperative Process for the Practicing Clinician." *The William & Mary Educational Review* 5, no. 1 (2018). https://scholarworks.wm.edu/wmer/vol5/iss1/11.

O'Brien, Nancy. "Reflexivity: What Is It, and Why Is It Important in Your Community?" University of Minnesota Extension, October 4, 2021. https://extension.umn.edu/community-news-and-insights/reflexivity-what-it-and-why-it-important-your-community.

CHAPTER 2

A Treasured History: Stories of Resilience

By Kristina Whiteman

"MY LIFE HAS CHANGED as I've realised that I don't actually have to have it all together. It is okay to be broken ... God uses broken vessels, so that we can shine out of his glory and not from ourselves. I think initially, we tend to think of missionaries as having it all together."

"But in reality, we are the broken ones that God is working on and through. I've become much more aware that our ministry is made up of broken people, and that we are all completely dependent on God .... I'm learning to show grace to myself and to others. My relationship with God has grown as I realise that he loves and uses broken people."

– Australian/New Zealander serving in Eastern Asia for 15 years.[1]

I spent a great deal of my life believing that being *a good global*

---

[1] All quotes from global workers come from *the Resilient Global Worker Study*: Written Interview. For more information, consult: Kristina Whiteman, "A Treasured History: Listening to and Learning from Global Workers' Stories of Resilience," (PhD diss., Asbury Theological Seminary, ProQuest Dissertations Publishing, 2023), 30525920.

It is not infallible heroes who are effectively crossing cultures for the sake of the gospel.

worker meant continuing no matter what and doing so with perfect faith and grace. The older I get, the more I realize that this myth of the *unflagging champion of the gospel* is a lie. It is not infallible heroes who are effectively crossing cultures for the sake of the gospel. Instead, God chooses to use ordinary people – people who have been broken and repaired through the gold of God's love. In their resilience, they have bounced back as his beloved co-laborers toward the *shalom* of God's kingdom.

The Resilient Global Worker Study

In 2017, my husband, Geoff Whiteman, created the *Resilient Global Worker Study* (ResilientGlobalWorker.org). He hoped to have 100 surveys, interview a few people, and write a neat little article from his research. Instead, 892 eligible people took the survey, and 247 global workers and former global workers participated in the written interview. In these interviews, they offered their time, wisdom, and honesty in over 600 pages of stories. Talking about this great gift with Geoff one day, I realized I needed to delve more deeply into these narratives to share nuggets of gold like this one from a North American who has served in Western Asia for nine years:

> God and I are like old friends on a porch, rocking back and forth. He knows me, and he sits beside me in gentleness. We can talk about all we've done together. There is a comfort. He is good to me. My approach to ministry has changed – I'm less hurried. I'm not rushing. I don't feel responsible. I also

know no matter what I do, God will make it work for better. He will overcome any brokenness in any person I serve. He's done it for me. He will do it for them. I just show up and be faithful and he will work it out.

My calling was to show up and be faithful. I honored the gift of these stories by delving deeply into them with a full analysis in my dissertation. Throughout the process, I asked: What can we learn from global workers' stories of how they have become more resilient?

One of the keys to my understanding of resilience is that it has both protective and responsive aspects. Grit is part of resilience (it's a *protective factor*), but another part of resilience is bouncing back to face adversity again through *responsive factors*.

I think this is best illustrated by the central metaphor we use for resilience: the Japanese art of *kintsugi*. In this artform, a piece of pottery which has cracked is repaired with gold. It reminds us that brokenness is not a shame to be discarded, but a treasured history to be honored. We are more beautiful through having been broken, and the places of greatest beauty in us are those places where we have experienced wounding and healing.

To take a deep dive into global worker stories, I used a theoretical framework called *narrative inquiry*. It gave me several lenses through which to look at workers' stories: relationship with God, interaction, place, and temporality.

As I have spent over 900 hours reading, absorbing, coding, and analyzing these stories, here is what I have found. Resilient global workers seek redemption in adversity. They receive themselves, others, and their situations under the care of a faithful God who has called them and will sustain them as they join his mission in the world.

The Lens of Relationship with God

It is impossible to understand global workers' journeys toward greater resilience without looking at their relationship with God. God is at the heart of these stories of resilience. Most workers connect growth in resilience to their spiritual growth and a deeper relationship of trust in and dependence on a faithful, strong, and good God.

God's calling to participate in his mission of love is fundamental to global worker resilience, as is God's transformation in their lives. These workers say that the very core of their being – their identity as God's *beloved* – is both a source and a result of the *resilience cycle* in their lives.

For many resilient global workers, their relationship with God is not only a professional byproduct, but also a personal necessity. Their stories and their inner selves are centered on God, as God is the companion in their lament and the source of their joy.

A North American who has served in Melanesia for 18 years shared this, "My relationship with God has shifted away from *certainty* to *security* ... . It isn't dependent on external dogma, but on internal processes and spirituality that sustains me. And it is sourced in him ... . I view myself with much more grace."

WHAT CAN WE LEARN? Workers' trust in God is not blind, naive, unwarranted, or automatic. Those who are most likely to express this trust tend to be more experienced, older, and more resilient. In the same way that a person would earn trust by being dependable, faithful, and loving, God has earned their trust.

Secondly, the resilient global worker's relationship with God anchors and makes possible their experience and shapes who they are as human beings. Their spiritual growth moves them toward a stronger relationship with a sovereign, faithful, loving, good God brings them to the field, sustains and strengthens them, and ultimately transforms them at the core of their identity.

These are not just people working across cultures, they are Christ-followers engaged in *theosis* – becoming like Christ. And this theosis involves facing adversity, breaking, and bouncing back more able to face the next trial. This is all part of the work-

God's calling to participate in his mission of love is fundamental to global worker resilience, as is God's transformation in their lives.

er's transformation in Christ. Their relationship with God shapes their resilience to be so much more than an increase in grit.

The Lens(es) of Interaction

Many global workers' stories of growing in resilience center around different types of interactions – with themselves (intrapersonal) and with others (interpersonal). When they talk about intrapersonal interactions, workers describe their own attitudes, attributes, and actions that build resilience.

Their stories show that the life of resilience is a life of *acceptance*. They accept themselves, in their strengths and limitations. They accept reality, what is and is not their responsibility. And they accept a helpful theology, that all things are under God's care and that God's strength is made perfect in their weakness.

When they talk about intrapersonal interactions, we also see a significant counter-narrative. Some global workers do not experience enough intrapersonal support. Some struggle. Some say they are not resilient. And some do not describe resilience or growth in resilience in their stories. Not every worker is growing in resilience, and not everyone even sees that as a possibility in their brokenness.

For most global workers, though, building a life of acceptance contributes to successfully navigating life's tensions. Paying attention to their strengths and weaknesses and meeting their own needs through practical acts is the way they find freedom and grace. Receiving the very things that are difficult enables them to also receive the "gold that fills the cracks."

"I think I have a more honest view of myself," explained a North American worker who has served in Southeastern Asia for 11 years. "I see my weaknesses, but don't feel I need to cover them. I think I am better at embracing my weaknesses and seeing them as opportunities for others to come alongside me and fill my weakness with their strength. ... I am more open to letting others help me since I've experienced the wonder and freedom that comes when they do."

Global workers also described what I call *transitional interactions*. This is when an internal change becomes external as it changes a worker's relationships with others. Greater understanding of themselves often becomes greater understanding of others. Greater grace with and for themselves often becomes greater grace for others through greater love, authenticity, empathy, encouragement, or forgiveness. In this movement from inner to outer, these global workers exemplify the importance of trying to understand the perspective of the other. The life of resilience is also a life of *empathy* for self and for others.

As workers told their stories of interacting with others (interpersonal interactions), there was a great duality. Other people may be a significant stressor, but they are certainly also global workers' greatest supports.

Global workers received support from people in the field and from people at *home*. Often they mentored workers, helping them to be or do better than they could have on their own. And sometimes they walked alongside workers in their real lives as companions for the journey. Whatever the relationship type, global workers say they thrive when they have long-term relationships with safe people in different roles who will pray for them, listen to them well, and accept and encourage them.

A North American who has served in Eastern Europe for 19 years described it this way: "For us, our greatest support has come from teammates or other missionary friends on different fields. Their *get it* factor and trusted friendship has enabled them

The conflict described by many global workers was not destructive conflict.

to speak life, truth, and comfort like few others."

Many of us have believed that conflict is one of the biggest negative issues that global workers face in the field. And it is true that in describing their interactions with others, interpersonal conflict came up a lot. Although this theme taps into the *conventional wisdom* that workers *biggest* problem is other workers, what we see in these stories is also that this doesn't *have* to be the case.

The conflict described by many global workers was not destructive conflict. There is hope that they can come through clashes and disagreements having built better relationships with others than they could have without the *iron sharpening iron* of constructive conflict.

One North American who served in South American for more than 30 years explained how she felt about being told that broken relationships between missionaries was a major cause of missionaries leaving the field.

"My reaction at that time was, 'How can that be? We're Christians, called of God...,'" she shared. "Yet, within six months of arriving on the field, I was involved in a conflict with another woman that created issues between our families as well as conflict among the team members. After a time, God worked in both our hearts, and we were reconciled and since that time, our friendship has grown."

WHAT CAN WE LEARN? What we see in these stories of interaction is that a life of resilience is a life of acceptance, empathy, and supportive relationships. Acceptance allows the intentional pursuit of those postures and practices that will become responsive

What we see in these stories of interaction is that a life of resilience is a life of acceptance, empathy, and supportive relationships.

and protective factors in their resilience. When global workers accept themselves and their lives both in their capacity and their constraints it creates vulnerability – but it also opens the way to empathy for others and the opportunity to freely give grace as they have freely received it.

In addition to acceptance and empathy, resilient global workers need other people. They need others who will listen to them with loving acceptance, pray for them, encourage them, and affirm their calling for the long haul. They also benefit from the capacity to engage with others through healthy boundaries and constructive, not destructive, conflict.

The Lens of Place

As they talk about their growth in resilience, workers also use themes of place – the physical location and the location-bound cultural milieu in which they live and work. First, global workers describe place-based adversity. Although the details of the challenges they face differ, there is one common element: the difficulties of language and culture acquisition. Many also face physical, mental, and relational health issues. Environmental strains that make life more hazardous or difficult are also significant for many.

But (surprisingly to me!) many global workers also experience place-based strength. The more they understand their context, the more fully they can minister there. Their difficult experiences can be a stepping-stone to greater resilience, rather than the end of the story.

"My thinking and beliefs have changed simply because the longer I am here the better I understand the beliefs of the host culture," wrote a North American who had served in the Caribbean for five years. "I have changed the way I address issues by starting from the vantage point of the host culture rather than my own."

WHAT CAN WE LEARN? Understanding context is key for ministry. Both workers and the people who care for them need contextual knowledge. We need to know enough about the challenges workers will encounter in the different categories of adversity to help them prepare for and face up to inevitable difficulties in ways that are both protective and responsive.

Although this is not the case for everyone, for many global workers place-based adversity can be a stepping-stone, not a hindrance, to resilience. These workers stories don't stop with health challenges, cultural challenges to their values, difficult relationships, crime, civil war, heat, or deportations. Rather, these things are mentioned because they are a stop along the way, an example of how God is at work to redeem all things for his glory and for the sake of his beloved people.

The Lens of Temporality

Global workers used themes of temporality (the interplay between past, present, and future) to talk about growing in resilience, often through redemption sequences. In "redemption sequences," the storyteller acknowledges the negative experience (something bad really *did* happen).[2] However, later in the story the teller says

---

2 Dan P. McAdams, Jeremy J. Bauer, Ellen P. Sakaeda, Beverly R. Anyidoho, Louise C. Machado, Jennifer M. Magrino-Failla, Maria C. K. Nicol, and Kenneth C. Phillips, "When Bad Things Turn Good," *Journal of Personality and Social Psychology* 83, no. 3 (2002): 602–610, accessed July 1, 2023,

that the negative has been redeemed in some way by a later experience or later processing. For many global workers, this is a way of making meaning from what they've experienced.

Also for many workers, these sequences are part of a cycle of growing more and more resilient. They experience something that breaks them, and then when they bounce back they find that they can handle more (they have more protective resilience). When they go through the next breaking adversity, they again bounce back (with more responsive resilience) even better in some ways. And they discover that, again, they have greater capacity (they grew even more in protective resilience). I refer to this as the *resilience cycle*.

The resilience cycle is like a spiral staircase. Although workers may sometimes feel like they are seeing the same walls of breaking and healing, they are moving higher and gaining new perspective even in repeated adversity. They see the difficult things that happen in their lives as part of a process, one which includes spiritual, emotional, and professional growth. These global workers know that the past prepares them for the present and the future in a way that redeems all things.

This positive journey has increased their desire to help others. They actively pass on lessons and hope that brings redemption to suffering. Most workers described growing in resilience. For them, the balance of lament and joy allows the pain of the past to hold meaning in the present and hope for the future.

A North American worker who served in Eastern Africa for around 30 years described the Lord providing two images after a time of difficulty. "One was a sunflower growing out from under a port-a-potty. This was real life growing into something beautiful in spite of, and maybe because of, the difficulty of where it was placed. ...God helps us grow even in the *crap*. He helps us filter out the negative and gives us good, lush nutrients to continue to grow even in the midst of difficulty. And the way we grow isn't

https://journals.sagepub.com/doi/10.1177/0146167201274008.

Workers grow into resilience over the long haul.

just mediocre in all of the difficulties, but it produces something beautiful that brings him glory."

WHAT CAN WE LEARN? Global workers become resilient. The goal for sending organizations cannot be to choose the people who are at the top of the stairs, but to support people as they climb. Workers grow into resilience over the long haul. This means that we must think about how to support people in that process, in ways that genuinely build resilience, step-by-step, for the long haul.

We must see redemption sequences for what they are – the balance of lament and joy, of grief and gratitude. It is enormously tempting to skip to the end, to the ultimate meaning-making we as Christians find in Christ and his resurrection. However, just as the story of redemption includes the suffering of the Cross, a redemption sequence includes pain.

It is impossible, in fact, to move forward without acknowledging our brokenness. We have to get past the moment where all we can see is the cross ... not by avoiding it but by going through it. We must grieve our losses, repent of our shortcomings, and own our heartache. Having lamented, we can turn toward gratitude for the ways that God is redeeming our loss. With the Psalmist, we can go from "*How long, Lord? Will you forget me forever?*" to "*But I trust in your unfailing love; my heart rejoices in your salvation. I will sing the Lord's praise, for he has been good to me*" (Psalm 13).

Implications for Member Care Practices

It is vital to recognize the beautiful fruit that the resilience cycle has borne in so many lives. Global workers' experiences go beyond breaking adversity. These are stories of growth, grace, freedom, strength, authenticity, and hope.

Resilience is also both a grace and a skill. As a skill, it can be practiced, increased, and built up. Workers can be encouraged to strive for the attitudes, seek the attributes, and work out the actions of resilience. They can also be trained in the skills necessary for good relationships.

Conflict competence, empathetic communication, and thoughtful teamwork – all these can become part, not just of the preparation and training of the individual global worker, but also of an organizational ethos that grounds their life on the field. In all these areas of resilience skill, global workers and those who care for and about them can recognize that it takes intention and work to avoid the bad and pursue the good.

As a grace, resilience is also more than the effort we put into it. The grace of resilience, not just for global workers, but for all of us, must be received from God. This movement begins with the acknowledgement that we are not now what we hope to become and that we are not able to face breaking adversity alone. It includes turning toward God and simply asking that the resilience of the resurrected Christ would be imparted to us. Resilience is an undeserved gift that God chooses to bestow, and we long to receive.

The next implication I see in these results is primarily for those who lead, equip, send, and care for global workers. We must acknowledge what is and what is not our responsibility. Like global workers, we must accept our own limitations, the reality of the systems in and from which we operate, and the preeminence of God's work in mission.

Member care workers are often less important in a worker's day-to-day life. It's our job to equip workers as well as we can, and to intervene in special circumstances. However, we also encourage and release them to find the support they need in the field from others. This tertiary role does not mean, however, that those who send global workers are not important. We can be

We have to get past the moment where all we can see is the cross ... not by avoiding it but by going through it.

safe leaders, long-term companions, and calling-confirmers. We can be available to hear workers' stories. We can listen to them and support them as they make meaning in their lives through narrative.

Finally, this research led me to conclude that all of us who care about global workers and want to see them thrive can learn from them to embrace the tension that is resilience. There is a temptation, especially in the Christian community, toward a toxic positivity that insistently puts a *silver lining* on bad things in an effort to make them disappear.

To whitewash the pain involved, or to claim that the resilience cycle is universal, cheapens both resilience and people's experience of it. Not everyone is progressing in their resilience, and even for Christians, not all suffering is redeemed this side of heaven. And even when adversity leads to growth, this does not mean that loss, trauma, loneliness, and brokenness have no long-term consequences or negative effects.

AND YET ... There is hope. In the stories of these global workers, we see that trust and dependence can be based in experience, not in denial. In their lives, we see the continuing possibility of resilience. We also witness that pain happens, but on the other side we *can* find beauty. Rather than being a shame to be discarded, brokenness can become a treasured history to cherish.

Resilient global workers acknowledge and accept the current reality, and they also have ultimate faith. Resilient global workers have picked up their cross to follow Christ. It truly is a *cross*, one which will inevitably lead to pain and suffering, to being crucified with Christ.

AND ... Resilient global workers look forward, believing as the apostle Paul expressed in Romans 6:5 that, "if we have become united with him in the likeness of his death, certainly we shall also be in the likeness of his resurrection." These workers claim that, "if we died with him, we will also live with him" (2 Timothy 2:11). They trust that, "through the cross, joy has come into all the world" (Resurrection Matins of the Orthodox Church).[3]

Each of us who follow Christ can learn from resilient global workers. We hold the pain of the cross, and we turn toward the hope of the resurrection.

This is true resilience.

KRISTINA WHITEMAN is an Orthodox Christian and resilience research-er who is passionate about God's mission in the world. Kriss and her husband, Geoff, have been married since 2003, serving in vocational ministry since 2000, and supporting global workers since 2007. She has published several articles on Orthodox missions and global worker care and is currently working in a staff position for Asbury Theological Seminary (asburyseminary.edu).

---

3 The full hymn can be found in The Paschal Hours, available at https://orthodoxprayer.org/Paschal%20Hours.html.

Questions for Reflection

- Think of a time when God sustained you in your ministry and/
  or life. What happened to keep you going? What practices
  allow you to turn toward God for comfort, healing, and
  empowerment?
- How can you nurture acceptance, empathy, and support for
  yourself and others in your life? How can you reach out for
  acceptance, empathy, and support from others?
- Who do you know who embodies true resilience? What about
  their life and/or ministry makes you see them as being
  resilient?

Additional Resources

Whiteman, Kristina. *A Treasured History: Listening to and
  Learning from Global Workers' Stories of Resilience.* Doctoral
  Dissertation, Asbury Theological Seminary, 2023. Available
  on ProQuest or by request from author.

CHAPTER 3

Top Ten Reasons For Missionary Attrition

By Andrea Sears

WHEN IT COMES TO MISSIONARY LONGEVITY, we have a *Goldilocks and the Three Bears* situation. Some stay too long, some don't stay long enough, and some stay for a period of time that is "just right." How do we know what the right choice is?

How Long is Long Enough?

A mission *term* is an arbitrary administrative invention that may or may not reflect the time required to become skilled and productive. Depending on the work, where it is done, linguistic/cultural learning curves, and characteristics of the missionaries themselves, the time needed to accomplish goals will vary greatly.

No one used to expect missionaries to return to their sending nations. The somewhat romanticized idea that they packed their belongings in a coffin and bought a one-way ticket had truth to it. Missionaries would often stay in their country of service until they died. Given the risks and dangers, that might not be very long. Those brave men, women, and children laid the groundwork in hard places for the completion of the Great Commission.

Today's mission perspectives look different. Our models are less colonial. We recognize the importance of empowering locals and not creating dependency on foreign missionaries. To do this well, staying indefinitely is likely not advisable.

This changing landscape brings a hard question for missionaries (and their agencies): when am I *done* with my mission? This is a very individual question for which no one right answer exists. Finding the answer requires discernment and prayer by missionaries and by those who support and advise them. Still, things may not happen on our expected timelines!

At the same time, high turnover rates are causing disruptions on teams, setbacks in mission work, and limited productivity. Given the time, money, and talent invested in missions, we have a stewardship responsibility to make sure that it results in maximum effectiveness to the glory of the Lord.

Between 2017 and 2022, I researched missionary attrition including surveying 739 former missionaries about the influence that certain experiences had on their decision to return home. These are the top ten reasons that missionaries leave the field that emerged: (1) burnout, (2) too little missionary care, (3) anxiety and depression, (4) team issues, (5) stress/instability, (6) health, (7) discouragement, (8) loneliness/isolation, (9) traumatic experiences, and (10) family considerations.

Past research has attempted to draw firm lines around each of these issues as *preventable* or *non-preventable*. However, even many health and family issues (typically deemed *unpreventable*) are *preventable* with the right kind of selection, preparation, and support.

As we examine each of these challenges, I encourage member care professionals and mission leaders to re-think the preventable/unpreventable paradigm. Where can we do better for our vulnerable kingdom workers? We may be unable to completely control certain factors, but we are able to influence them to varying degrees.

This changing landscape brings a hard question for missionaries (and their agencies): when am I done with my mission?

Burnout

Of the 59% of missionaries that affirmed the statement "I experienced burnout," 44% said it influenced their decision to return home.

Family, team, health, cultural, financial, and spiritual issues can add up to take their toll on a missionary's stamina. If we don't provide missionaries with resources to address that toll, serious distress and burnout can result from pushing themselves too hard for too long. It's true that the workers are few and there is much work to do. But the way forward is not asking the few to work themselves to the point of exhaustion and breakdown. Who will do the work then?

Too Little Missionary Care

Of the 71% of missionaries that affirmed the statement "I received too little missionary care," 53% said it influenced their decision to return home.

This sentiment seemed to apply to sending churches, mission agencies, and friends/family support networks alike. Maintaining long-distance relationships of care is difficult, and doesn't often happen. Those not trained in missionary care don't necessarily

Self-sacrificing people may put themselves last for too long and cross the threshold into long-lasting depletion.

know how to offer support, because they do not understand what the missionary is experiencing. This leaves family, friends, and sending churches under-equipped to supplement agency care efforts.

While larger agencies have more resources for member care, smaller agencies may not be able to provide much support once missionaries are on the ground. And included in this challenge is self-care: are we encouraging and facilitating missionaries to care for themselves? Self-sacrificing people may put themselves last for too long and cross the threshold into long-lasting depletion.

Anxiety and Depression

Of the 58% of missionaries that affirmed the statement "I, my spouse, or my child suffered from anxiety," 41% said it influenced their decision to return home.

Of the 62% of missionaries that affirmed the statement "I, my spouse, or my child suffered from depression," 42% said it influenced their decision to return home.

The chronic stress of missionary life provides fertile ground for anxiety and depression. Cross-cultural living involves significant loss of control. The accompanying feelings of uncertainty, powerlessness, and frustration can combine into hopelessness.

Missionaries know that their ultimate hope is in God, but this does not mean that they don't experience unwanted emotions in their day-to-day lives. These can add up and lead to longer-term coping difficulties. This does not mean that they are weak or that they aren't good enough Christians. But the continuing stigma in the church about mental illness may result in missionaries being reluctant to share these struggles and seek help. If they do look for help, resources may not be available to them.

Team Issues

Of the 70% of missionaries that affirmed the statement "There was a conflict on the team," 45% said it influenced their decision to return home.

Yes, conflict can be a problem in every relationship, and missionary teams are no exception. What's different about these relationships is that they usually need to meet both professional and social needs. This creates unique relationship pressures that most people don't experience in the same way in their home nation. When asked what caused conflicts, participants shared several common themes including sin/dysfunction, leadership styles, communication problems, differences in boundary setting, and allocation of resources.

Of the 48% of missionaries that affirmed the statement "I felt that some of my team members/leaders lacked integrity," 30% said it influenced their decision to return home.

Several factors can create this impression. Lack of supervision/ accountability on the mission field can create an environment in which opportunities to compromise integrity are tempting and numerous. Loneliness and homesickness, as well as people in local communities that see perceived benefits to having relationships with foreigners, can push missionaries to seek inappropriate companionship.

Some misguided leaders turn to dishonesty as a means to keep wrongdoing under wraps and "protect the name of Christ." Finally, cross-cultural interpretations of integrity can differ. Each team member may wish to acculturate to differing degrees with local standards of integrity. Team members from other cultures may also view integrity differently. Either of these scenarios can create suspicion among team members.

Of the 62% of missionaries that affirmed the statement "My team members did not meet my expectations," 40% said it influenced their decision to return home.

Expectations greatly color our perception of an experience and may be unmet for various reasons. They may not have been set appropriately, clearly communicated, or acknowledged. Common sources of unmet expectations included leadership, integrity, conflict, abrupt/frequent staffing changes, personality or life stage differences that made it hard to connect, communication, jealousy, control, and personal dysfunction.

The team's expectations of women (or women's expectations of how they will contribute on the team) may be unclear or unrealistic. Singles and families may have differing expectations about the roles they will fill in each other's social lives. Conflict often results when expectations are not met.

Of the 57% of missionaries that affirmed the statement "I struggled to understand my role on the team," 39% said it influenced their decision to return home.

Of the 50% of missionaries that affirmed the statement "My job responsibilities did not meet my expectations," 32% said it influenced their decision to return home.

A significant number of missionaries experience ambiguity or dissatisfaction in their role. One common concern was that their

A significant number of missionaries experience ambiguity or dissatisfaction in their role.

role changed when they arrived on the field, or it fit poorly with their skills and background.

Many reported that they had a workload that was too great or too small, or that their role was poorly defined or unnecessary. Others felt "put in a box" (they were not free to innovate or expand their role), restricted in their duties because of gender, or received inadequate direction from leadership.

Of the 47% of missionaries that affirmed the statement "I did not feel at liberty to pursue my passion and call within the team/agency that I was a part of," 31% said it influenced their decision to return home.

Some missionaries felt this because of a poor fit between their skills/passion and their role. Others thought that tasks outside of their gifting took so much time that there was little left to engage in the ways in which they felt called.

Still others believed that their call evolved when they got to the field, but their team's vision of what they needed done did not. Some wanted to innovate ministry methods, but their conservative leaders and organizations did not. Remaining highly engaged while enduring these challenges while also bearing the hardships of the missionary life may not feel worth it.

Of the 38% of missionaries affirmed the statement "I was no longer sure of my calling (or my spouse was no longer sure of his/her calling)," 25% said it influenced their decision to return home.

The mission field attracts service-oriented and driven people who may struggle to say no and set appropriate boundaries.

Most missionaries do their work because they believe the Holy Spirit moves them to engage in particular ways to build his kingdom. They view their work as God-directed rather human-directed.

In the same way that a call takes missionaries to the mission field to begin with, a change or diminishing in the call can take them on to the next phase of God's plan for them. What's key is discerning whether their restlessness comes from themselves or God.

Stress

Of the 67% of missionaries that affirmed the statement "Frequent transitions caused a lack of stability," 43% said it influenced their decision to return home.

Change is constant in cross-cultural life. Instability causes distress, and when it affects central aspects to daily life, its impact increases. Missionaries living cross-culturally experience drastic changes: for example, the language they use, the climate they live in, and the diseases endemic to their area.

Their social support network gets a complete overhaul: new neighbors, a new work team, a new church, and a new social community. Then further surprises occur. Mission vision and priorities may shift, affecting job responsibilities. Housing situations change, causing family upheaval. Unexpected emergencies strike, turning life upside down. Turnover on the team may create a heavy workload for those remaining, begetting burnout, and then more turnover.

Of the 60% of missionaries that affirmed the statement "It was difficult to set boundaries on what was demanded of me," 37% said it influenced their decision to return home.

The mission field attracts service-oriented and driven people who may struggle to say no and set appropriate boundaries. This couples with a prevalent expectation that missionaries should be willing to sacrifice everything for their work building the kingdom of God.

This can lead to poor work-life balance (workaholism), a lack of self-care, and the erosion of family life. Loneliness can lead to poor boundaries with social media and technology. Team differences on boundaries can result in conflicts. Cultural concepts of appropriate boundaries also differ from place to place and can contribute to culture stress.

Health

Of the 68% of missionaries that affirmed the statement "I felt that stress affected my health," 48% said it influenced their decision to return home.

Of the 50% of missionaries that affirmed the statement "I felt that stress affected the health of others in my family," 34% said it influenced their decision to return home.

Of the 52% of missionaries that affirmed the statement "I experienced significant health problems," 30% said it influenced their decision to return home.

The Social Readjustment Rating Scale (SRRS) measures stressful life events in the last year. A score of 200 is high, with half of people suffering serious physical illness as a result. At 300, one is almost certain to be hospitalized within two years. The typical missionary has a score of 600. First-term missionaries average about 900.

This scale is proven to predict health outcomes: the more stressors, the more likely a person is to become ill. Missionaries suffering the effects of double or triple the level of maximum manageable stressors will experience higher rates of physical illness and higher need for counseling and other emotional support services.

Discouragement

Of the 84% of missionaries that affirmed the statement "I experienced discouragement," 59% said it influenced their decision to return home.

Varied and sustained stressors over time add up to discouragement. When missionaries pour so much of themselves out for others with little in return, it is nearly inevitable that discouragement will result. The work is hard and the fruit is rarely immediately visible or measurable. Going up against entrenched worldviews and intense spiritual bondage is exhausting and does not always feel victorious.

Isolation/Loneliness

Of the 73% of missionaries that affirmed the statement "I felt isolated/lonely," 50% said it influenced their decision to return home.

Many missionaries reported feeling that they were "out of sight, out of mind" – forgotten by those who sent them off to the field with fanfare. Compounding that is the fact that in their country of service, authentic cross-cultural relationship building is difficult and slow. People may have ulterior motives for wanting to get

When missionaries pour so much of themselves out for others with little in return, it is nearly inevitable that discouragement will result.

close to Western foreigners, including a perceived financial benefit. Language/cultural differences make it harder to genuinely understand one another and increase the likelihood of offense/conflict. Feeling disconnected from their former support network, but not yet having built a new one, leaves the missionary vulnerable to intense loneliness.

Traumatic Experiences

Of the 36% of missionaries that affirmed the statement "I had a traumatic experience not covered above (robbery, assault, and death of a family member were specifically queried in previous questions)," 21% said it influenced their decision to return home.

Trauma is a lasting emotional response to a distressing event or series of events. Missionaries often live in high stress environments. They may stand out in their settings, which can make them targets for harm or threats of harm. They may walk with others through traumatic experiences, leaving them with secondary trauma.

Sudden, even life-threatening, illnesses or accidents may strike them or those they care about. Political violence or instability may create fear and a heightened state of alertness with a potential need to evacuate. Even the daily experience of struggling to understand and be understood, not give offense, navigate

One of the most unpreventable factors that brings people home is family care, particularly elder care and children's education.

unfamiliar or unfriendly systems, get formerly *simple* tasks done, and get along with team members who are equally stressed can become traumatic. Trauma marks us and molds our future emotional responses to certain situations.

Family

Of the 50% of missionaries affirmed the statement "I wanted to be close to my aging/ailing parents," 36% said it influenced their decision to return home.

64% of missionaries (who were parents) that affirmed the statement "There was a lack of options for my child/children's education," 39% of parents said it influenced their decision to return home.

One of the most unpreventable factors that brings people home is family care, particularly elder care and children's education. Children have needs that may be harder (or impossible) to meet on the field. Parents age and need care, and missionaries are often the type of nurturing people that step up to care for them.

Conclusion

These categories are interconnected and overlapping. For example, work-life imbalance causes burnout, mood disorders, team conflict, health problems, and family issues. A lack of missionary care contributes to burnout, team issues, loneliness, discouragement, and family difficulties. A lack of human resources creates team and role stress that in turn impacts health problems, discouragement, and burnout.

Stress is a common denominator across these findings. We may not be able to eliminate it, but we can manage it and minimize its impact by equipping missionaries with the ingredients necessary for resilience. Diverse stakeholders have a role to play. Each is equipped to address different pieces of the puzzle. For example, a mission agency may not be able to address missionaries feeling forgotten by those back home, but a sending church and friends/family certainly can. A sending church can do little about team or role issues, but a mission agency can.

The reasons for turnover stem from all stages of the missions process: from how we talk about missions in church, to recruiting and selection, to training and preparation, to launch, to on-field orientation, to long-term maintenance and care. Solutions will need to permeate every phase of the process as well.

So what do we do now? This research reveals where challenges lie. Further study can help determine effective solutions, and how and by whom they can best be applied. Together, we can better support missionaries, increase their longevity, and help them to reach that *just right* point for their call and the mission organization's needs.

ANDREA SEARS was a missionary in Costa Rica for 13 years working with the poor in the largest immigrant squatter settlement in Central America. She and her husband founded giveDIGNITY (give-dignity.org), a Christian community development ministry that she still directs from the US. It focuses on the educational, vocational, and spiritual growth of community members. Andrea holds a master's in intercultural studies with a specialization in community development.

Questions for Reflection

- When you talk about missions in church, are you realistic about struggles or do you perpetuate a super-hero myth of workers that are impervious to challenges because of the strength of their faith?
- What commonalities do you see linking the 10 challenges in this chapter? Who can affect them (who are the various stakeholders with control/influence over these challenges)?
- How can you make sure you send the right people for the job, team, and culture?
- How can you prepare missionaries adequately for what they will face in crossing cultures?
- What part can you play in helping various stakeholders come together to create a synergistic effort in missionary care?

Additional Resources

Brierley, Peter W. "Missionary Attrition: The ReMAP Research Report," in *Too Valuable to Lose: Exploring the Causes and Cures of Missionary Attrition*, William D. Taylor, ed. William Carey Library, 1997.

Hay, Rob, et al, eds. *Worth Keeping: Global Perspectives on Best Practice in Missionary Retention*. William Carey, 2007.

O'Connor, Mavis. "ReMAP II – Retaining Missionaries – Agency Practices: Older Sending Countries in Europe and North America."

Rains, Hailie. "ReMAP II – Retaining Missionaries – Agency Practices: Newer Sending Countries from Africa, Asia and Latin America."

Sears, Andrea D. "Missionary Attrition Survey 2017." Full results published online at themissionsexperience.weebly.com.

Van Meter, Jim. "US Report of Findings on Missionary Retention." World Evangelical Alliance, December 2003.

CHAPTER 4

Trauma Informed Staff Care

By James Covey

EVIDENCE OF A TRAUMATIZED WORLD IS EVERYWHERE — difficult and overwhelming events fill our newsfeeds and occur regularly in our communities. As the global church sends workers to live and serve cross-culturally, especially in more demanding locations, the possibility of workers becoming traumatized amplifies.

Trauma can happen as the result of exposure to intense and challenging experiences. Additionally, because historical traumas can impact people in a variety of ways throughout their lives, difficult and complex environments also increase the likelihood of traumas from the past becoming triggered and activated.[1]

Everyone sits next to their own pool of tears, but we often don't approach people with that perspective. Organizations and individuals caring for the wellbeing of cross-cultural workers need to know how to respond to this aspect of trauma. This starts through understanding trauma and how to care in a trauma-informed way.

---

1 The "CDC-Kaiser ACE Study" proved a cause and effect correlation between childhood trauma and physical or emotional problems in adulthood. Centers for Disease Control and Prevention, "About the CDC-Kaiser ACE Study," https://www.cdc.gov/violenceprevention/aces/about.html.

Everyone sits next to their own pool of tears, but we often don't approach people with that perspective.

What is Trauma?

Many different definitions of trauma exist. Someone might say the traffic on the way to work or putting parents in a retirement community was *traumatic*. Then the same word may be used to describe being evacuated under gunfire from South Sudan while watching neighbors and friends being killed.

Trauma can also be challenging to define because it is an experience not an event. A difficult or stressful event does not mean it was *traumatic*. Each person's individual experience of events can be different, even if they witnessed the same event. For example, in Rwanda the post-genocide prevalence of Post-Traumatic Stress Disorder (PTSD) among the survivor population is 25%. While this is incredibly high, many people who experienced the same event never developed PTSD.[2]

The book *Healing Teens' Wounds of Trauma* describes three principles of wellbeing: the world makes sense, justice is available, and I am a person of value.[3] Those are all broken in some

---

2 C. Musanabaganwa et al., "Burden of Post-traumatic Stress Disorder in Postgenocide Rwandan Population Following Exposure to 1994 Genocide Against the Tutsi: A Meta-analysis," *Journal of Affective Disorders* 275 (2020): 7–13, https://doi.org/10.1016/j.jad.2020.06.017.

3 Margi McCombs, James Covey, and Kalyn Lantz, *Healing Teens' Wounds of Trauma: How the Church Can Help, Facilitator's Guide* (New York: American Bible Society, 2018).

way by trauma. The impact increases when this happens in formative years.

Psychiatrist Bessel van der Kolk defines trauma as "not the story of something that happened back then, but the current imprint of that pain, horror, and fear living inside [the individual]. ... These events leave us stuck in a state of helplessness and terror, and results in a change in how we perceive danger."[4] The book *Healing the Wounds of Trauma Facilitator Guide for Healing Groups* refines this adding that trauma "... can be caused by a single event, a prolonged event, or repeated events.[5]

A variety of factors affect an event's impact, and its potential traumatic outcome. Those influences can include personality, community support, and pre-event factors such as previous traumas dating as far back as childhood. Each can increase or decrease the chances of a trauma experience resulting from an event.

How Does Trauma Affect Us?

Trauma happens when our brain, bodies, and emotions re-wire to continually mobilize for threats. When this occurs, the brain's functions responsible for impulse control, judgment, and executive functioning turn down.[6]

The brain's fight, flight or freeze responses are helpful when we are in danger – for example, an aggressive bear attacking us – but not helpful when we're not. These maladaptive brain shifts can leave people stuck. They may react in ways they don't understand or intend, and this can be made worse, often unintentionally, by

4 Bessel van der Kolk, *The Body Keeps the Score: Mind, Brain, and Body in the Transformation of Trauma* (New York: Penguin Books, 2014).

5 Harriet Hill, Margaret Hill, and Richard Baggé, *Healing the Wounds of Trauma: Facilitator Guide for Healing Groups* (Downers Grove, IL: IVP Books, 2009).

6 Nadine Burke Harris, "How Childhood Trauma Affects Health Across a Lifetime," YouTube video, 17:47, posted by TED, December 14, 2015, https://youtu.be/95ovlJ3dsNk.

Hyperarousal

Excess Energy: Anxiety, Anger, Overwhelmed,
Chaotic, Rigidity, Compulsiveness, Stuck ON

Fight / Flight

Working with
a practitioner
can help
expand your
tolerance.

Window of Tolerance

Grounded, Flexible, Open Curious,
In Control, Present, Emotionally Regulated

Stress and
trauma can
shrink your
window
making it
easier to be
thrown off
balance.

Hypoarousal

Lack of Energy: Depression, Disassociation,
Disconnection, Autopilot, Withdrawn, Shame, Stuck OFF

Freeze

the people living around them.[7]

Normally after a crisis our body returns to a state of calm with our top-brain (cortex) back in control operating what Psychiatrist Daniel Sigel describes as our *window of tolerance*.[8] Trauma impacts a person's whole system from how memories are stored (differently when under high stress) to how they react when any part of their bodies perceive danger.

When someone has been traumatized, the window of tolerance

7 Harris, "How Childhood Trauma."

8 Daniel J. Siegel, *The Developing Mind: How Relationships and the Brain Interact to Shape Who We Are*, 3rd ed. (New York: Guilford Press, 2020).

can shrink considerably causing phases of hypo or hyper-arousal. Hyper-arousal is an elevated state of energy – *fight* or *flight* mode. It can cause anxiety, angry outbursts, an increased heart rate or breathing, elevated blood pressure, or panic. In contrast, hypo-arousal is the *freeze* mode. It causes the body to shut down, resulting in emptiness, depression, or numbness.[9]

Many things in life can result in us leaving our window of tolerance: kids misbehaving, being cut off on the highway, being belittled at work. People with trauma experiences are more easily triggered out of their window.

Anything that reminds us of a memory, an event, or a person in the past is called a *trigger*. These triggers are usually aroused through one of our five senses. For example, the smell of Christmas dinner being cooked could trigger good memories of a grandmother. Hearing a dog bark could cause a person's heart to beat fast because it triggered a memory of getting bit.

When someone struggling with trauma encounters a trigger, it reminds them both consciously and unconsciously of something painful. The whole body responds, and it may take time for their brain, body, and soul to settle back down. Trauma also spiritually shapes them, but the question is *how* is that spiritual formation happening?

Armoring up and *hunkering down* are common automatic trauma responses which can negatively affect their relationship with God, themselves, and others. It can also invite them to drag God into the courtroom of our experience instead of taking their experience into the courtroom of God.[10]

---

9 National Institute for the Clinical Application of Behavioral Medicine, "How to Help Your Clients Understand Their Window of Tolerance," accessed March 1, 2023, https://www.nicabm.com/trauma-how-to-help-your-clients-understand-their-window-of-tolerance/.

10 J. Campbell, "Trauma Informed Spiritual Formation," speech presented in 2023.

How Do Traumatized People Behave?

A traumatized person may perceive the world as a dangerous and scary place. This can come to the surface when people experience events like evacuations, war, robberies, unexpected transitions, or the sudden death of a loved one. It can also be true for those with historical and unhealed traumas. Trauma symptoms are as varied as the types of people and events that happened. We also need to take culture into account because reactions to events differ across cultures.

One way to describe the experience for the survivor of trauma is alarmed aloneness. The event that caused trauma may be shameful, hidden or even repressed to the point that people may be unaware that they are experiencing a triggered trauma.[11] Bessel van der Kolk refers to engaging traumatic memories as the unbearable heaviness of remembering, complicated by the fact that traumatic memories are often disorganized.[12] We typically try everything we can do to not remember trauma which makes these improperly stored memories even more *dis*integrated.

People with disorganized and disintegrated memories from a historical trauma may not be aware they are being triggered or reacting in a self-protective way. This lack of awareness prevents them from seeking help and people around them from trying to avoid triggers.

I worked with someone who had a traumatic and violent experience in high school. Throughout his adult life he never allowed himself to talk about his trauma nor experience any sadness or grief. He was terrified of what these might do to him, so he avoided them. It left him unable to empathize with his family, friends and colleagues on issues related to sadness, loss, transition, or grief.

---

11 To go deeper on this topic read Frauke C. Schaefer and Charles A. Schaefer, eds., *Trauma and Resilience: A Handbook* (Frauke C. Schaefer, MD, Inc., 2016).

12 Van der Kolk, *The Body*, 195.

One way to describe the experience for the survivor of trauma is alarmed aloneness.

Instead, he came across as cold and uncaring. When someone shared about a difficult emotion, he went cold and blank, but was unaware of his response. He was mystified by his trouble developing close relationships with co-workers and experienced a lot disconnection and dissonance in life. After dealing with his trauma, he began to feel empathy and connection with his family and his co-workers. They found him more accessible, vulnerable, and this increased their ability to trust him.

There is also evidence that trauma remains in the system of families, teams, and organizations even beyond the events that occurred. Generational trauma was initially studied in the children of holocaust survivors. Even though they did not witness the traumatic experiences of their parents, they still had many of the behaviors or symptoms of trauma.[13]

This area needs more research in the context of cross-cultural work and teams. However, it is helpful to be aware that particular groups or teams that have experienced trauma can – through their behavior, attitudes, and beliefs – pass on unhealthy trauma symptoms to a team or organization.

How we respond to concerning behaviors we see matters. Care needs to be taken to not overattribute or minimize the possibility of trauma history. People struggling with relationships, anger, depression, or anxiety, or even those creating HR nightmares and exploding teams, may be traumatized or have other mental

---

13 Diane Langberg, "Trauma Healing Institute 2018 Community of Practice - Diane Langberg · Opening Presentation," Trauma Healing Institute, April 6, 2018, video, 1:21:31, accessed August 28, 2021, https://youtu.be/w9N49JvP_Fw.

Shifting from the question "What's wrong?" to "What has happened?" grows grace and allows for a broader spectrum of possibilities.

health problems. Either way, approaching people with kindness and grace can help deescalate a situation so that the source of the behavior can be better understood.

What is Trauma Informed Care?

A large mitigating factor against getting traumatized is community support.[14] Being with people in the moments of crisis is a profound opportunity to bring healing amidst critical events or the triggers that are brought on through them. This is why having a trauma informed approach to member care is so important.

Research into trauma informed care started as an effort to help medical professionals effectively respond to traumatized patients. This was especially important for first responders dealing with people in emergencies. These discoveries can inform and equip anyone in caring domains.

According to the Institute on Trauma and Trauma Informed Care, "Trauma-Informed Care understands and considers the pervasive nature of trauma and promotes environments of healing and recovery rather than practices and services that may inadvertently re-traumatize." It emphasizes a shift in focus from "what's

---

14 "What Trauma Does to Your Brain and Body | Bessel van Der Kolk," The Well, January 26, 2022, video, 51:15, https://youtu.be/ZKa7V_mV8l8.

wrong with you" to "what *happened* to you." [15]

When people demonstrate behavior that challenges those around them, it is easy to jump to the conclusion that something is wrong with them. But when organizations focus on finding what is *wrong*, they can trigger trauma histories which can worsen a situation and bring harm to others involved. Even care providers in cross-cultural organizations or churches may find it difficult to not *fix* what is *wrong* in the moment.

Shifting from the question "What's wrong?" to "What has happened?" grows grace and allows for a broader spectrum of possibilities. It considers the negative impact of life experiences as opposed to the negative attribution of something being wrong. This approach has potential to improve "... engagement, treatment adherence, health outcomes, and provider and staff wellness."[16]

The stress of cross-cultural situations, particularly in locations with frequent violence, can increase trauma propensity in workers coming from disruptive backgrounds or places. To care for these workers well, a trauma informed care model needs to be followed by more than just care providers. This way of thinking must permeate the people and systems that make up our churches, ministries, and cross-cultural organizations. It is key to holding cross-cultural workers accountable for their actions but do so in a caring way with space and time to process.

But what does a trauma informed care approach look like? I've created a model complied from a variety of research-based

---

15 Institute on Trauma and Trauma-Informed Care, "What is Trauma-Informed Care?" University at Buffalo School of Social Work, accessed March 1, 2023, https://socialwork.buffalo.edu/social-research/institutes-centers/institute-on-trauma-and-trauma-informed-care/what-is-trauma-informed-care.html.

16 Caelan Menschner and Alexandra Maul, "Key Ingredients for Successful Trauma-informed Care Implementation," (Rockville, MD: Substance Abuse and Mental Health Services Administration, 2016), accessed March 1, 2023, https://www.samhsa.gov/sites/default/files/programs_campaigns/childrens_mental_health/atc-whitepaper-040616.pdf.

trauma informed care practices in the fields of medicine, refugee support, and adolescent care. It contains five steps:

- Increase Trauma Awareness
- Provide Safety
- Empower People to Make Choices
- Focus on Strengths
- Understand Roles and Make Referrals

These steps can guide any individual or organization towards a more compassionate resolution to the difficulties that arise when a person's trauma is triggered. And it may also help the trauma-tized person make steps toward healing including expanding their window of tolerance once again.

INCREASE TRAUMA AWARENESS. The first and most important step is to understand is the prevalence of trauma and grow in aware-ness of the personal and systemic impact trauma can have on individuals and organizations. Trauma impacts people regardless of country of origin or service, culture, or faith background. It impacts physical, emotional, spiritual, and mental health. In dif-ficult situations, it can also cause self-protective or *hunker down* responses.

A critical part of a trauma informed staff care approach is attentiveness to how people behave who have experienced traumas. It is difficult to build psychological safety with team members that believe that people cannot be trusted or that others are *out to get them*. They may constantly react in defensive and sometimes aggressive postures because their brain is telling them they are not safe.

Knowledge of these trauma characteristics enables systems to be developed to allow for a response that avoids re-triggering trauma. For example, colleagues, staff care facilitators, and administrators can be trained to enter difficult conversations or personnel situations with a humble and soft approach asking

It is difficult to build psychological safety with team members that believe that people cannot be trusted or that others are *out to get them*.

questions geared towards understanding what is beneath the surface of behavior. This may create a culture shift for navigating all forms of people care and not just situations with trauma-related behaviors.

PROVIDE SAFETY. The second step is to provide physical and emotional safety.[17] Avoiding triggering individuals who have experienced trauma supports them staying in or even expanding their window of tolerance. It also reduces the self-protective attitude and behavior of *people are out to get me or harm me*. Regardless of trauma histories, for teams to thrive, it is essential that people feel psychologically and physically safe in order to express themselves, take risks, and not have trauma re-triggered. Training and implementing psychological safety practices can be an important part of this.

Avenues for people to report (whistleblowing) and power reduction systems or advocates in place who can find out safety thresholds will help create environments of greater safety. For example, a male supervisor or HR representative may let their female staff member choose the location or someone they trust to be with them for difficult conversations. However, misuse of power

---

17 Amy Baker, "What is Trauma Informed Care?" accessed March 1, 2023, https://www.oregon.gov/oha/HPA/DSI/QHOCMeetingDocuments/5-8-2017%20 Learning%20Collaborative%20Trauma%20Informed%20Care.pdf.

Much of trauma is centered around an experience that took power and control away from an individual.

and a history of systems not being followed can take safety away.

EMPOWER PEOPLE TO MAKE CHOICES. The third principle is to empower people to make choices whenever possible. For the care provider this is critical in a crisis response and when providing trauma informed care. Much of trauma is centered around an experience that took power and control away from an individual. Yet people with trauma may find making decisions difficult.

As a result, it may be natural for care providers to conclude that removing choices will help. However, this can trigger a person's trauma because they feel out of control. Instead care providers can offer a few easy choices that give those they are caring for control over their own care.

Questions that provide choices can help. Here are a few examples:

- Would you like to come to me, or can I come to you?
- Would you like to meet a counselor in our organization, or can I recommend a counselor elsewhere?
- Would you like to talk more about this, or is there someone you trust you can talk to?

FOCUS ON STRENGTHS. A strengths-based approach builds on the empowerment principle. It notices and encourages the strengths a person used in the past to manage difficulties.[18] A sense of physical, mental, emotional, spiritual, and social stability is needed for a traumatized person to feel safe. Stressful cross-cultural field settings are often a source of instability, which makes noticing and encouraging strengths even more important.

Focusing on strengths helps un-armor, affirm, and encourage the parts traumatized people need to navigate an environment that may be triggering their trauma histories. Focusing on strengths can also reduce or avoid shame that can come up when unhealthy behaviors are recognized or pointed out.

UNDERSTAND ROLES AND MAKE REFERRALS. Everyone needs to know and communicate their role, as well as know who else with other skills can help. Member or staff care providers have a variety of training, education, and background. Some are counselors, trained spiritual directors, crisis and peer debriefers, or mentors.

Administrators and supervisors in field environments also provide care to those reporting to them. In certain organizations, they may be the only member care support available. In fact, it is often a supervisor or field coordinator who first notice potential trauma responses in their staff.

A further complicating factor is that in a given situation the people needing care often go beyond just a struggling individual. Others on their team, their supervisor, or others may all need attuned attention. But in a team conflict, for example, who is the staff care provider supposed to attend to? What if the team includes married couples or people living in the same neighborhood?

It's important to note that when dealing with trauma, unlicensed care providers and administrators are not equipped to process a person's trauma. That is best done in a therapeutic setting. However, community support is critical. They can support

18 Menschner and Maul, "Key ingredients."

59

trauma healing in other significant ways. If everyone knows their role or purpose, they can respond to care needs, including ones involving trauma, as a holistic team.

From the beginning of a care interaction, it is important for care providers to affirm the challenge and then clearly articulate what they offer and provide referrals for other necessary parts of care they do not. Here are examples:

> "It sounds like this has been a difficult transition. As a spiritual director, my role is to accompany you in your relationship with God through this challenging time. I also know a person with extensive experience in your country of service who had a similar situation on arrival. Would you be interested in receiving peer mentoring from them?"

> "Wow, this sounds really hard! You would be welcome to share more about your experience of your team member with me. My training in debriefing has equipped me to be a good listener. As a coach, I could also come alongside you to ask helpful questions about steps you can take to navigate this difficult relationship. If you would like to work on ways this relationship is triggering for you, I can recommend a counselor."

Trauma Recovery

Untreated trauma can be triggered throughout life and lead to unexpected and unintended complications for a traumatized person, as well as their friends, family, and colleagues. A trauma informed approach to care recognizes how wide-spread trauma is and engages with people in ways that invite healing for the deep wounds of the heart, mind, and soul.

Just like significant physical wounds, it takes time, treatment, and care invested by the individual who is wounded and those joining their caring team. But through this, we have a unique

If everyone knows their role or purpose, they can respond to care needs, including ones involving trauma, as a holistic team.

opportunity in our shared *called-ness* to contend for these co-laborers.

People who have experienced great suffering can demonstrate the healing that happens through Christ and the community with whom he has invited us to live and serve. Their journey to wholeness welcomes all to join them in experiencing the healing power of Christ.

JAMES COVEY holds a master's in marriage and family counseling and is a licensed professional counselor supervisor from Texas. He has been serving with SIL International (sil.org) since 2011 living in Kenya, then in North Africa, and now resides in Malaga, Spain. He co-authored *Healing Teens' Wounds of Trauma, Facilitator Guide and Teen Journal.* He has a podcast called "Shop Talk with Brandi and James" on issues of health and wellbeing for cross cultural workers.

Questions for Reflection

- How is your window of tolerance and when was the last time you were out of it? What was your trigger? What tools help you move back into your window and how could you coach someone else who is often outside of theirs?
- What are situations, people or conflict you have been aware of that may have been complicated by unknown trauma reactions? How might you use the *trauma informed care* approach next time to manage that situation differently?
- What are particular systems, structures, or policies you have in your organization that help staff feel safe? If you don't know who could you talk to in order to find out more or advocate for better practices.
- What referral resources do you have for someone with a trauma history?

Additional Resources

Ergenbright, Dana, Stacey Conard, and Mary Crickmore. *Healing the Wounds of Trauma: How the Church Can Help* (*Facilitator Guide for Healing Groups*). American Bible Society, 2021.

McCombs, Margi, James Covey, and Kalyn Lantz. *Healing Teens' Wounds of Trauma: How the Church Can Help*. American Bible Society.

Schaefer, Frauke C., and Charles A. Schaefer, eds. *Trauma and Resilience: A Handbook* Frauke C. Schaefer, MD, Inc., 2016.

Siegel, Daniel J. *The Developing Mind: How Relationships and the Brain Interact to Shape Who We Are*. The Guildford Press, 2020.

Van der Kolk, Bessel. *The Body Keeps the Score: Brain, Mind, and Body in the Healing of Trauma*. Penguin Books, 2015.

CHAPTER 5

The Place of Welcome

By Celeste Allen

A RECURRING THEME OCCURS IN NOVELS of quests and adventures. At some point, after the heroes have traveled far and battled many foes, they come to a place of refuge. In that place, they are fed, cared for, and allowed to rest. Often, they receive wise counsel before they continue their journey. Like many – or even most – literary themes, this has reflections in Scripture.

In 1 Kings 19, we find Elijah, who has fought long and hard for the Lord's glory. In response, Jezebel has effectively put a price on his head. So, Elijah runs for his life and finds himself in the wilderness.

An angel came, touched him, and said, "Get up and eat." He looked around, and there by his head was some bread baked over hot coals, and a jar of water. He ate and drank and then lay down again. The angel of the Lord returned a second time, touched him, and said, "Get up and eat, for the journey is too much for you." So, he got up and ate and drank. Strengthened by that food, he traveled forty days and forty nights until he reached Horeb, the mountain of God. There he went into a cave and spent the night. And the word of the Lord came to him: "What are you doing here, Elijah?" (1 Kings 19:5–9).

While most missionaries may not think of their lives as either heroic quests or epic journeys, providing pauses for rest remains a critical part of caring for global Christian workers. In *The Jesus Way*, Eugene Peterson notes that "we stop, whether by choice or through circumstance, so that we can be alert and attentive and receptive to what God is doing in and for us, in and for others, on the way."[1]

Elijah needed to experience the hospitality of being fed and allowed to rest before he could come to an emotional and physical place where he could tell his story, meet with God, and move forward. The same is true for Christian workers. They also need to stop in a place of refuge and be strengthened for their journeys.

Why Hospitality?

On the most basic level, resilience is what keeps missionaries on the field. Resilience allows missionaries to persevere and even thrive in the face of disappointments, ministry setbacks, disconnection from friends and family, and all manner of losses. A key to resilience is self-care. A missionary who cares for herself, body and soul, is a missionary who can stay the course. Receiving hospitality is one vital aspect of self-care.

As our world grows increasingly war-torn, there is a real need for places where Christian workers can escape violence and experience rest and restoration. As we face one of the greatest refugee crises in history, those who work with refugees need opportunities to catch their breath and find respite. As more and more environmental disasters hit our world, there is a greater need for places where aid workers can go to restore their souls. As immigration controls tighten, workers finding themselves expelled from their countries of service need places to regroup and process their experiences.

What all these people need is hospitality. A pause to be

---

1 Eugene Peterson, *The Jesus Way: A Conversation on the Ways That Jesus Is the Way* (Wm. B. Eerdmans Publishing, 2007).

A missionary who cares for herself, body and soul, is a missionary who can stay the course.

refreshed and gain a new perspective can make the difference between long-lasting, productive ministry or burnout, an early departure from the field, or grim, exhausted labor.

Whether Christian workers are in personal crises that require specialist help, or they are simply tired and in need of rest to avert a personal crisis, missionaries need hospitable and safe spaces to rest and be refreshed. Places that are free from distractions can help them hear God's Spirit, feel his peace, and rest in him.

Offering missionaries hospitality can take away some of the burdensome details of life like deciding what to eat, shopping, cooking, cleaning up, etc. It frees up time, space, and energy, allowing missionaries to focus on healing and deepening their relationship with the Lord.

"Hospitality makes member care more effective," shares Karen Howe of Oasis Rest International. "Compare eating dinner on the run (scarfing down a sandwich while driving to the next thing) to sharing a meal with family or friends, seated around a table. Either way you're fed, but the first may result in slight indigestion and a desire for more. The second will result in full digestion (you'll get all the nutrients possible from the food) and a satisfying memory."

In both scenarios, you've accomplished the same task. However, the second one is much more effective, especially in the long run. Receiving member care in the context of hospitality does the same thing.

"Hospitality creates the space/context for someone to fully receive the care," Karen further explains. "Member care can be done without hospitality (and that may be what is needed at times to just get through a situation), but sustainable member care needs to include an element of hospitality." [2]

In his book, *Reaching Out*, Henri Nouwen says, "Hospitality is not to change people, but to offer them space where change can take place." [3] When member care providers offer hospitality, it shows the missionary that she isn't just an anonymous client but someone who is known and loved, someone who can feel safe enough to be open and vulnerable. It is in that place of welcome and safety that the weary soul can find rest and God can begin to work in the missionary's heart and life.

How Do We Do Hospitality Well?

So, what does hospitality as a means of member care look like in the twenty-first century?

Returning to the account of Elijah in 1 Kings 19, note that the angel of the Lord first cooks for Elijah. Then he gives him physical comfort through touch. And lastly, he normalizes Elijah's situation. He assures Elijah that his physical exhaustion is to be expected and that rest and refreshment are appropriate before continuing to the next phase of his life.

Often the first step of hospitality as member care is meeting the missionary's physical needs: food and shelter. While we could pitch a tent and hand over a slice of bread, that doesn't quite reflect the welcome we would offer if Christ were coming to visit.

In *Making Room*, Christine Pohl says, "In hospitality, the stranger is welcomed into a safe, personal, and comfortable place, a place of respect and acceptance and friendship. Even if only briefly, the stranger is included in a life-giving and life-sustaining network of relations. Such welcome involves attentive

---

2 Karen Howe, correspondent, email message to author, February 9, 2023.

3 Henri J. M. Nouwen, *Reaching Out: The Three Movements of the Spiritual Life* (New York: Image Books, 1986).

listening and a mutual sharing of lives and life stories. It requires an openness of heart, a willingness to make one's life visible to others, and a generosity of time and resources."[4]

Sometimes workers don't need counseling or debriefing. They may not even need someone to host them. They simply need a place, prepared with love, where they can rest and hear from God. Providing that means intentionally creating a hospitable environment.

While it is better to offer the hospitality of a fold-out bed in the family game room than to offer no hospitality at all, people are usually most comfortable when they have their own space. A designated area the worker can call his own – whether that be a bedroom, a guest wing, or an apartment or house – is important.

However, creating a space for hospitality entails more than just providing four walls and a bed. People can go to a hostel for that. Beyond such obvious factors as clean, comfortable bedding, washed or vacuumed floors, and dust-free surfaces, true hospitality anticipates the needs of guests.

Having both a fan and extra blankets in the bedroom allows for guests with differing internal thermostats. Having tissues in the bedrooms (or in every room since you never know where tears will flow) is helpful. It's good to keep a small supply of toiletries on hand in case the missionary forgot something.

A neat and uncluttered environment makes it much easier for a guest to be at peace. Small touches such as a welcome sign with the missionaries' names let them know they are seen. Subtle accents add beauty, but it's important to beware of overkill. For example, one tasteful calligraphy of Scripture on the wall is nice. Four can feel like the biblical equivalent of a room full of motivational posters!

Additionally, people feel safer and more cared for when they understand their environment and know they can be warm and

4 Christine D. Pohl, *Making Room: Recovering Hospitality as a Christian Tradition* (Michigan: Wm. B. Eerdmans Publishing Co., 1999), 13.

True hospitality is not a matter of putting on an impressive display. Rather, it's about welcoming people into a space where they can experience God's love and welcome.

well-fed. Guests need to know where they can find what they might need and what their boundaries are. For example:

- Where are glasses or mugs if they want a drink?
- Where can they find a snack if they want one?
- Are they free to move throughout the building at night?
- Can they adjust the temperature of their room?
- Are any places off-limits?

Considering special needs is also important. Ask guests in advance if they have allergies or sensitivities. This not only avoids awkwardness but helps workers feel cared for. It is vital, once we gather this information, to pay attention to it. A welcome plate of chocolate chip cookies might excite a family, but a worker with diabetes will not be blessed by it. And if your guest tells you she is intolerant of tomatoes, serving spaghetti Bolognese will not make her feel heard. Providing good food for people with sensitivities and allergies can be challenging, but doing so communicates love and concern.

In cases where a missionary is in a hosted hospitality space, the host must make every effort to connect well with the guest. Whether the host is a professional member care provider or a caring volunteer, offering hospitality to the missionary *is* member care. Attentiveness and an attitude of welcome show workers that the host is interested in them and their life experiences and desires their good.

When a missionary arrives, she is asking herself, "Can I trust these people in my fragility?" The first meal, shared graciously and generously without hurry, can answer that question. The missionary gets to know the hosts in a comfortable way and understands that she's come to a place that's quiet, caring, and makes no demands. Before any formal member care meetings take place, she can breathe deeply and change her pace.

True hospitality is not a matter of putting on an impressive display. Rather, it's about welcoming people into a space where they can experience God's love and welcome. Neatness counts, but people are more at ease in a home that feels lived in than one that feels like a museum. Save the heirloom china and cut glass for personal use and bring out the IKEA tableware so the missionary mom can relax as her kids eat.

In her book *Table Life*, Joanne Thomspon notes, "Hospitality is more about your faith than your competence. ... [S]haring your table isn't fueled by faith in your magnificent entertaining skills or gregarious personality; it's believing that God will satisfy hearts as well as appetites when you share your table in Jesus' name."[5]

One critical part of not just hospitality but every aspect of member care is ensuring that those offering care are, themselves, well cared for. Just as field workers can only pass on what they have to those they serve, member care providers cannot offer what they don't have. If guests sense that the member care provider lacks peace and calm, they may not feel safe or may even feel they need to care for the carer. Therefore, those providing hospitality need to protect their margin and their spiritual life.

Scheduling back-to-back guests with no downtime in between, engaging with guests from early mornings through late nights,

---

5 Joanne Thompson, *Table Life: Savoring the Hospitality of Jesus in Your Home* (Minnesota: Beaver's Pond Press, 2011), 12.

or racing into the morning with guests at the expense of taking our own time with the Lord can lead to those offering hospitality suffering the very burnout they are seeking to combat in missionaries. All these things may be necessary on occasion, but for a sustained ministry, they cannot be the norm. Self-care cuts both ways – missionaries and member care providers both need it.

Being the Hands and Feet of Jesus

Not every organization has the resources or calling to provide its own hospitality house, but every mission organization can cultivate a culture of hospitality as part of member care. This kind of culture values individuals as well as their work. And it recognizes that the generosity God poured out in welcoming us to his table is the same generosity that needs to be expressed in welcoming his workers.

This can begin with agency staff sharing hospitality with one another and their local Christian community. It can include welcoming missionaries not only to the agency's office but into staff's homes. Additionally, sending agencies that offer member care at their offices can partner with local churches to find parishioners willing to provide hospitality for visiting missionaries. This invites local believers to become part of the care of missionaries and expands their vision and understanding of sharing God's kingdom.

Some training may be necessary – both for staff and local believers. That needs to be grounded in an understanding that hospitality is a matter of expressing Christ's love through generosity rather than putting on a show. They will also need to understand appropriate member care boundaries. This guidance can help them see the gift they can offer, whether they have a large space or a one-bedroom apartment.

We can also display hospitality in member care without necessarily providing a place to stay. The angel of the Lord didn't give Elijah a bed, but he did care for him. Similarly, hospitality in member care includes more than just offering a bed. Jesus had

Some hospitality ministries have had great success sending practitioners to train Global South missionaries and pastors while also learning from them.

no home of his own. Nevertheless, he welcomed people with his very presence.

We, too, can exhibit a Christ-like welcome when meeting with missionaries in neutral spaces or even in their homes on the field. The attitudes displayed in graciously giving time, listening attentively, and even assisting in necessary tasks are all aspects of hospitality in member care.

Showing hospitality in a missionary's home might look like setting the table, helping with the washing up after a meal, or volunteering to read the little ones a story. Showing hospitality in a neutral space could include setting aside more time than you think you need so you can give the missionary your undivided and unhurried attention. If you're looking at the missionary, not at your watch or phone, that tells her she is valued rather than just an item on your to-do list.

With the growing number of Global South missionaries, care must be taken to offer culturally appropriate and affordable hospitality. This may mean utilizing or even establishing on-field hospitality venues or sending member care teams to specifically give hospitality as care.

Many non-Western cultures value hospitality more highly than Western societies. It would be worthwhile to investigate how churches in these societies practice hospitality not just for *honored guests* but for one another.

At the same time, Global South churches can sometimes

equate rest with laziness. Thus, education can help missionaries and agencies from Global South cultures understand how the hospitality they value goes hand in hand with sabbath rest. Some hospitality ministries have had great success sending practitioners to train Global South missionaries and pastors while also learning from them.

Can a mission agency raise funds to help underfunded workers access member-care hospitality venues? Is it culturally appropriate to do so? How can we support workers from any culture who want to practice hospitality as member care? What can we learn about hospitality from our Global South brothers and sisters? Addressing some of these questions can help global mission agencies and member care providers more fully care for all workers.

Whether in-house, on-field, or utilizing designated hospitality ministries, caring for missionaries through hospitality is a practical expression of being the hands and feet of Jesus because it is in the place of welcome that workers can find Christ's healing.

CELESTE ALLEN is a writer, retreat leader, and member care provider. A native of Pittsburgh, Pennsylvania, Celeste has been involved in international Christian work for more than thirty years, serving first in Asia, then in Europe. For 12 years Celeste hosted a hospitality house in Italy for people in Christian ministry. She now serves as a staff care worker with Oasis Rest International. Celeste's passion is to help people connect with God.

Questions for Reflection

- How can you foster a culture of hospitality in your organization?
- What local contacts can you make or resources can you find to help bring hospitality into your practice of member care?
- What key factors in the changing world affect how you/your organization practices (or can practice) hospitality?
- How can hospitality as member care be practiced for and by Global South workers?

Additional Resources

ORGANIZATIONS:

Daybreak Academy lists hospitality resources in Asia, https://daybreak-academy.org/member-care-centres-asia/.
Global Member Care Network has contacts for hospitality resources around the world, https://globalmembercare.com/.
Oasis Rest International provides hosted hospitality houses for people in ministry, https://www.oasisrest.org.
Member Care Europe lists hospitality resources online, https://www.membercare.eu/category/resources/retreat-centres/.

BOOKS:

Butterfield, Rosaria. *The Gospel Comes with a House Key: Practicing Radically Ordinary Hospitality in Our Post-Christian World* (Illinois: Crossway, 2018).
Pohl, Christine D. *Making Room: Recovering Hospitality as a Christian Tradition* (Michigan: Wm. B. Eerdmans Publishing Co., 1999).
Thompson, Joanne. *Table Life: Savoring the Hospitality of Jesus in Your Home* (Minnesota: Beaver's Pond Press, 2011).
Wrobleski, Jessica. *The Limits of Hospitality* (Minnesota: Liturgical Press, 2012).

CHAPTER 6

Caring in the Way of Christ

By Vernon Salter

TOM PASTORS A MEDIUM-SIZED CHURCH in a major denomination. While not part of a significant sending denomination, his church sends more missionaries than the average. He sat at his kitchen table to discuss a couple who had returned early from their third assignment and were not returning overseas. Their anger and accusations towards the denominational leadership confused Tom.

When I asked him, "What have you heard from their US-based denominational leaders?" he said, "Nothing. They haven't contacted us." It became clear that Tom's church doesn't regularly communicate with the mission leaders responsible for sending people overseas. Moreover, Tom's confusion revealed he had expectations for those leaders – that they would care for the people he sent them. That seemed normal and natural to him. Hence his confusion.

Those unmet expectations reveal not just a communication gap but a culture gap between Tom's church and the sending agency. This is one of numerous potential gaps in the network of relationships required to form, train, care for, and develop overseas Christian workers. Each gap corresponds to an area of potential resilience in cross-cultural workers. People like this couple are our brothers and sisters, even our friends, and their

Certain aspects of member care areas are so significant that not investing in them is more costly than providing them.

potential resilience and longevity often goes unaddressed and undeveloped.

In the past 10 years, thousands of Western missionaries have come off the field earlier than their agreed terms.[1] Statistically, more than 35% of Western missionaries serving in the decade before 2018 returned home early.[2] Some came home for unforeseeable family issues. Others returned for predictable, even likely well-known, reasons. A number came back to serve as leaders back home. Most left because of crises – relational, systemic, or environmental.

Missionaries, like the couple sent by Tom's church, woke up one day and realized, "I can't do this anymore." They did not have the ability to bounce back from what happened, which is resilience. Hard, complex things left them overwhelmed and hopeless.

What is true for individuals working cross-culturally is also systemically true for agencies and care givers. Certain aspects of member care areas are so significant that not investing in them is more costly than providing them. In this case, this means we need to recognize the high value of certain activities that prepare and care for cross-cultural workers.

As I have listened to sending agencies, church leaders, and

---

1 Andrea Sears, "Research with Permanently Returning Workers from the Field," Research Findings (2018).

2 Sears, "Research."

care givers over the last few years, the consensus is, "We thought we were doing well preparing and caring, but now we don't know." Some leaders talk about their expectations for their role versus others' roles in missionaries' lives. Others mention lacking resources to develop and care for their friends and colleagues. Most share about not being aware of their missionaries' needs, plans, or expectations.

> "How are Millennials responding to the presence of care in an organization? In the past, it was considered helpful but not necessary. Now effective care is the number 1 issue in organization choice for overseas service. It is so significant, that they will change organizations (or quit), within the first 2 years if adversity is experienced and care is not available."[3]

This all attests to the need for one overarching kingdom reality: truly relational collaboration. Kingdom collaboration doesn't work apart from quality relationships. To relate well, we must soberly recognize the financial, time, and opportunity costs of not doing so. To pursue collaboration, these relationships must be biblical in their culture, multidisciplinary in their partnership, and open-handed in their posture.

Factors that Oppose Collaboration

Collaboration isn't easy, and two cross-cultural work realities oppose it: complexity and societal shift. The complexity of relationships between any agency, church, and missionary is often confusing. No universal set of developmental tools, postures, or plans can solve this. Missionaries are sent out at the end of a

---

3 Geoff Whiteman, "How Organizations Can Best Support Resilience," Research Findings (2021).

series of complex decisions. They receive this complex network's outcomes without the decoder ring to understand what those decisions mean.

This makes preparation for the field murky. Responsive care often reduces to a shotgun approach at best. As a care giver, I can't universalize care for cross-cultural workers from all agencies. My care efforts only function as well as my ability to recognize the humanity of the person in front of me. Sending agencies and sending churches also cannot apply the same care strategies to everyone.

The other factor impeding quality collaboration is societal shift. As close relationships suffer in the modern Western world, society continues seeking technological answers to well-being. However, this process fails as a strategy for personal development. "Technology is a brilliant expression of human capacity. But anything that offers ease everywhere does nothing (well, almost nothing) to actually form human capacities."[4]

As family integrity fades, tools and screens replace relationships. Our preparation model for missionary service has become more cognitive and behavioral than relational. I wonder if this results from societal voices leaking into the kingdom for decades.

Has the certified, degreed, informational preparation model for missionary service replaced the way of Christ – a community-based, relational, and experiential model? If so, both the launching community and those being launched are broken. To repair the damage, we must collaborate over the well-being of our friends living and working cross-culturally.

Collaboration Reflects a Biblical Culture

Church elders, agency leaders, and care givers have a better model for addressing cross-cultural workers' ongoing formation and care needs. We can step back from shiny web pages and slick

---

4 Andy Crouch, *The Tech-Wise Family* (Grand Rapids, MI: Baker Books, 2017), 66.

When I believe that God's glory resides in people, I can see them as the valuable individuals God created them to be. I want to hear what God is saying to them.

tools to engage in the way of Christ. "If Jesus is God incarnate, then God chose to reveal himself in analog, not digital."[5] The way of Christ is relational and glorious, but it is also not easy.

Collaboration has key differences from cooperation. Cooperation is marked by a medium relational commitment and work-based trust. It tends to value roles over people. It focuses on organizations over collaborative communities, and on products over people.

Biblical collaboration embraces a relationally dense, high-trust community model. Collaboration engages through relationships and encapsulates God's glory. It is lasting and resilient. When I believe that God's glory resides in people, I can see them as the valuable individuals God created them to be. I want to hear what God is saying to them. I want to listen to God with them.

Recently, I heard a care agency board member explain that their first day of meetings only involves catching up with and praying for one another. The next day focus on business, but that only occurs after they spent time with each other in the Lord's presence. They are fostering a collaborative culture which is evident and spreads when they engage with people outside their team.

5 Scott McKnight, foreword to *Analog Church*, by Jay Y. Kim (Downers Grove, IL: InterVarsity Press, 2020), 2.

Collaboration Involves Multidisciplinary Partnership

When church leaders and agencies don't take advantage of relationships, key information gets lost in between. I am prone to live in my silo, offering one slice of care. Collaboration allows me to see agency culture, personal history, and previous care. It makes me aware of the whole and of how God is operating in everything.

Relational collaboration ensures that churches, sending agencies, and care givers more readily identify needs. Having identified the needs, they train and engage those areas more effectively. They also have more success integrating care and development processes.

Through Missio Nexus (missionexus.org), we've developed a multi-agency people care community that seeks to equip, advise, and support member care in agencies. Several of us spent time in 2022 crafting a description of collaboration as it applies to member care. We envisioned, "... member care not as a single department, but a series of connected relationships and areas of well-being throughout an organization and the sending church. Member care done well is inherently collaborative."[6]

As we considered the meaning of *organizational member care*, key elements emerged for us. The first was that organizational member care can never be the sole responsibility of a single organizational department. This recognizes that supporting people care and development is a holistic endeavor that touches on multiple areas of peoples' work and lives.

Another element that emerged was that care and development are made possible through collaborative relationships throughout an organization and the sending church. It is the product of organizational cultures that acknowledge the vital ways in which every department supports global workers.[7]

6 Kimberley Drage, personal communication, May 3, 2022.

7 Kimberley Drage, "The Role of Organizational Health on Members," presentation at Orlando, Florida, 2022.

Collaboration is an Open-Handed Posture

Collaboration requires an open system mindset – it can't be just me and my resources. Instead, it's you, me, others, and all that the kingdom makes accessible. A closed system says, "This is all I have." An open system says, "We have all!" God gives us all we have and provides for all our requests. We offer our resources freely in our collaboration, not just our organization.

The secular world often calls collaboration a *power sharing environment.* In secular collaboration, I have power and you have power. Sharing that power looks more like cooperation or a product delivery system. You have something I need, and I want enough relationship to ask for it. Cooperation relies on saturation, a broad audience.

In kingdom collaboration, all the power belongs to a third party. God, you, and me are involved, but God has all the power and glory. It begins only when it engages the glory of God through the way of God. That means we recognize that what we offer was never ours to begin with. Therefore, we offer it with open hands and humble hearts. Collaboration prefers a smaller community because it becomes more potent with relational connection and understanding.

Collaboration is also an organic filtering and targeting process. Our understanding of each other, the organizational culture, and how God is leading our partnership means we hear what (or what not) to do in our care collaboration. It happens more easily and automatically the more we know about one another. It takes relationship to customize what we bring, aiming it accurately at the intended audience.

John 8:50 says, "I am not seeking glory for myself; but there is one who seeks it, and he is the judge" (NIV). In our collaborative efforts, the way of Christ means ensuring that how we relate to each other, and the overall collaboration, both bring glory to God. When I collaborate, I am the servant of all in the collaboration circle. I see the value of each person and engage and maximize

What if we decided, today, to launch relationally dense collaborative partnerships to cultivate deep resilience among these dear ones?

their design. This, in turn, brings glory to God.

What if the way of Christ inspired us to give our resources so our fellow global workers are followed and cared for throughout their careers? What if we decided, today, to launch relationally dense collaborative partnerships to cultivate deep resilience among these dear ones?

When this process happens, we see churches that ensure agencies know what God has been doing in candidates' lives. We see care givers communicating to provide more holistic care. We also see relational connections deep enough that care givers can customize their efforts for their agency partners.

The investment for each person in a collaborative environment is so significant that it should feel like a group of friends who happen to be formed and aimed at kingdom purposes. You invest in people you know by name. It's deeper, not broader; holistic, not siloed; and long-term, not short-term. True collaboration feels like a community.

I contend that biblical collaboration feels like the kingdom of God. Since kingdom collaboration is kingdom activity, it should feel like the way of Christ. Both should involve relational activities and Holy Spirit-driven connections.

The Word of God should be shared. Encouragement and exhortation should be rich. The environment should be inviting. Collaborative relationships should be life-giving. As in your local body, there should be a sense that our relationships with one another are something beautiful we create together.

Like local body relationships, collaborative care recognizes the need to talk to and know each other before we partner. Conversations can start with, "I know that in other meetings, we might move immediately into business, but I'm wondering about how God is leading you in your family decision." Collaborative care recognizes the need to attend to the liminal space in our collaboration.

Recently I was sitting around a table with a special group of care givers, discussing their gaps in care. One of these sages said, "I sense that what God might be saying is ...." The whole table tuned in and listened for potential confirmation in their hearts. Listening to the voice of God together transforms our collaboration into a kingdom movement.

Choosing Collaborative Partners

At some point, we have to choose certain collaborative partners and not others. Choosing well means listening to God with our potential partners, and prayerfully assessing the correspondence of our values and skills. We probably don't need to collaborate with those whose giftings and resources match our own. We need complementary gifts – people who are strong where we are weak.

However, we also want collaborative partners who share our values. The things we treasure most should aim us in a similar direction. Once we have chosen collaborative partners, we need to see them as friends with whom God led us to collaborate. Knowing that quality relationships invite us into God's goodness, we plan our relational encounters to intentionally foster this. We go deeper, so our impact can be more potent.

A multidisciplinary care team is a good example of values and gifting dynamics. As a clinical counselor, I bring a certain gifting and competency. However, I am only one slice of the care pie.

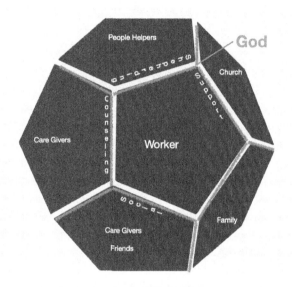

To care well, I need to partner with others more skilled in soul care and spiritual direction.

How we shape our care efforts matters. This starts with everyone involved believing that we are more effective and whole together as a care team than apart. If one person elevates themselves, our collaboration will not succeed.

Wouldn't it be wonderful if this same perspective on values and giftings was apparent in the collaboration between churches and sending agencies? What if an agency amplified their church partners' support and formation role? What if family members, friends, care partners and clinicians worked together with God to provide holistic care?

That might look a little like the above diagram which is based on Dr. John Warlow's pyramid of care,[8] and adapted to represent

8 John Warlow, *The C.U.R.E. for Life: Part One; God-Centered Transformation* (Australia: Ocean Reeve Publishing, 2017), 115.

the three-dimensional interconnectivity of member care. You can imagine the light gray lines as the golden thread representing God's presence connecting each area when we work in a kingdom collaboration way. This is what holistic and collaborative care looks like.

Collaborative Keys

Let's return to the couple we discussed in the beginning and consider collaboration from the lens of dilemma, process, and outcome. The dilemma is that people, like this couple, who are living cross-culturally face hardships that reveal their many forms of fragility. Unable to rebound in healthy ways, some break, fade, and drift back to their passport country lost and broken.

Maybe they needed to be formed deeper for the battle. Maybe their brokenness needed to be better processed and therefore honored in appropriate ways. Maybe their training for living and ministering overseas was inadequate. Almost certainly, they were too alone.

Even in a crowd of other servants, they felt disconnected, unsure, and unloved. Then one day, they realized their resources were low, and the expectations for saintliness were high. "I can make this work," they told themselves. Until the breaking day came when they couldn't anymore.

The process for resolving this dilemma is a relational one. Senders and care givers must provide substantial time to looking, listening, and learning. We must learn the realities of the work where people like this couple serve. Then we must look to the Lord and others around us to choose people and partners to meet those needs. We must keep people, like this couple, at the forefront of our minds as we collaborate on how we will prepare, respond, and consider the future impact of our efforts. We must do this together as care givers, churches, and agencies.

Finally, we must ask about the outcome. What do we want to see? We want collaboration among all the key players to produce a powerful culture focused on care and development. We want assessments to identify key personal development areas. We want a clear pathway to the preparation resources. When they arrive overseas, we want them to be connected to well-informed mentors who will bring the development areas together. We want the missionaries to know beforehand what their ongoing care resources are.

Collaboration is not easy. A commitment to it moves us away from our siloed care culture and brings real and radical change. In this desired future, sending churches feel deeply connected and aware of their sent ones' current realities. Sending agency staff experience being *with* many rather than *alone* among many. Care givers are able to flex and adjust care based on each person and situation's actual needs rather than hypothetical ones.

May we each highly value the treasure found in performing member care in the way of Christ. May we make the hard choice toward relational collaboration in the coming years!

VERNON SALTER is the director of care for Mission Training International (MTI, mti.org) in Palmer Lake, Colorado. He is also the co-owner of Smith and Salter Consulting (smithandsalter.com).

Questions for Reflection

- How have you framed your partnerships in more cooperative ways than collaborative ones?
- How does a cooperative framework create resistance to developing collaborative relationships?
- Where have you experienced kingdom collaboration?
- Where could you most easily start developing kingdom collaborative partnerships?

Additional Resources

Resilient Global Workers. *The Resilient Global Worker Study.* https://resilientglobalworker.org.

Warlow, John. *The C.U.R.E. for Life: Part One; God-Centered Transformation* (Australia: Ocean Reeve Publishing, 2017).

II · Engaging Our Changing World in Member Care

CHAPTER 7

Into the Fullness: Women in Mission Raised, Restored, Released

By Michele Okimura

ONCE UPON A TIME, there was a little girl in the closet. This closet was her favorite place to escape the chaos and violence going on around her. Yet, it was a lonely and dark place. She was hidden and unseen.

Yet God *saw* her.

From a young age, Jesus began to woo her out of that closet into his brilliant light and loving embrace, so he could show the world his glory.

This was my story. And in many ways, I believe it could be yours as well. Many, if not all of us, have our own closets, of sorts, made up of negative core beliefs, trauma, disappointments, pain, and shame that we may not even be fully aware of until the Lord shows us.

I love the rhythm of transformation as we follow Jesus. God continues to *raise* us up from any dark valley we ever have found ourselves in and builds us up. He *restores* us so he can *release* us into a greater fullness of who he created us to be and into our destiny. God has such a passion to see each of us healed, healthy, and holy! And this applies even more to people who care for others.

The Lord desires for all of us to be healed and renewed in our

The Lord desires for all of us to be healed and renewed in our minds, so we can walk boldly and confidently in our identity in Christ without hindrances or barriers!

minds, so we can walk boldly and confidently in our identity in Christ without hindrances or barriers! Let us demonstrate openness and intentionality in following the Lord's leading when dealing with any blockages and unhealthy patterns in our lives that we become aware of. Let us courageously reach out for help when needed through means such as professional counseling or prayer ministry even as we encourage others to do the same.

As a paraphrase, I love how The Passion Translation (TPT) expresses Romans 18:18–19: "I am convinced that any suffering we endure is less than nothing compared to the magnitude of glory that is about to be unveiled within us. The entire universe is standing on tiptoe, yearning to see the unveiling of God's glorious sons and daughters!"

Transformation is a process. Miracles of the heart and greater freedom in Christ await you, me, and those you serve. Your own breakthrough ripples out to your family, your ministry, and those you care for! But how do we do this? How do we proactively care for our own emotional and spiritual health and not neglect them in our care for others? How can we care for the garden of our own lives in such a way that we are thriving and able to give?

The following are just five of the many stepping stones that have helped me to step into the greater overflow of God's purposes and dreams for me.

Stepping Stone 1: Grow in Self-Awareness

The questions we ask ourselves matter. Asking the Lord to reveal what is in our own hearts is crucial because only God fully knows what is in our hearts. Being self-aware doesn't often come naturally for many people. It is a skill that must be learned, practiced, and developed.

Becoming self-aware makes it possible for us to make positive changes, make better choices, and understand ourselves. It can also help us improve our relationships, get in touch with our emotions, and respond to situations in healthy ways.

Here are some helpful questions you can ask yourself daily to grow in your self-awareness. Ask the Lord to help you answer them.

At the beginning of each day, ask:

- What attribute do I want to grow in today (for example patience or generosity)?
- What is one thing I really want to accomplish today?

At the end of each day, ask:

- What went well today?
- What did not go well – what could I do differently going forward?
- What did I learn today?
- What are 3 things I am grateful for?

If you had a concerning incident, you can ask yourself:

- Why did I react that way?
- How do I feel about that?
- Why do I feel this way? Does it remind me of a past experience? If so, what experience? Converse with the Lord if something comes to mind.

Stepping Stone 2: Embrace Your Identity

You are your Heavenly Father's beloved child. Yet many of us struggle at times to fully believe who God says we are. I have struggled with many negative core beliefs due to my past experiences – lies that God has helped me exchange for the truth of who *he says I am.*

As Paul writes in 2 Corinthians 10:5, "We demolish arguments and every pretension that sets itself up against the knowledge of God, and we take captive every thought to make it obedient to Christ." God cares about changing the automatic neuropathways of thinking in our brains that do not reflect his thoughts!

As you read the following statements, ask yourself if you believe them:

- I am God's chosen, beloved child.
- I am God's magnificent intention.
- I am a chest full of treasures and gems.
- I am a masterpiece being painted.
- I am a priceless gift given at the perfect time.
- I am significant, important, and have immense value.
- My intelligence sparks innovation and solutions.
- From a whisper to a roar, my voice is worthy of being heard.
- My compassion and kindness heals and restores.
- I am a beacon of hope, integrity, and justice.
- My prayers release angels on assignment.
- I soar with the strength of eagles' wings.
- I was born for such a time as this.
- My dreams matter to the heart of God.
- I am a glorious mystery being revealed.
- I have greatness in me that will bless the world.

Ask the Lord to reveal to you what negative lies you still believe about yourself so you can deal with them. There are many

God wants us to have a healthy self-love that is not arrogant, prideful, or narcissistic

Bible verses that describe your identity in Christ that you can meditate on.

Consider this paraphrase of Ephesians 2:10 (TPT): "We have become his poetry, a re-created people that will fulfill the destiny he has given each of us, for we are joined to Jesus, the Anointed One."

Stepping Stone 3: Love Yourself

Jesus said, "Love your neighbor as you love yourself." Matthew 22:39 (NLT). God wants us to have a healthy self-love that is not arrogant, prideful, or narcissistic. Continue to grow in fully loving yourself in the way God wants you to *so that* your capacity to love others increases significantly. If we love ourselves well, then we have the ability and capacity to love others well.

Due to experiencing abuse in my background, I struggled from childhood to well into my adulthood with great self-hatred and self-rejection. Through the years, I am so grateful to God to have experienced his healing touch and transformation.

God is quite creative in how he heals, restores, and renews us. He can touch us through prayer, counseling, a movie scene, Scripture, a person, a song, art, or through a circumstance... and so much more.

In 2022, I attended a retreat with just a few women at my friend Nancy Vuu's home. Nancy surprised us one day, telling us we would be getting our hair and makeup done, have a professional photo shoot, and would be going to a special dress-up dinner at a fancy restaurant wearing beautiful crowns she had given each of us! I happened to be the first one who finished getting my hair and makeup done, so I got dressed in my pretty dress earlier than the others.

Nancy, who is always full of ideas, beckoned me outside to her porch where there was a large mirror leaning against the wall. She told me to go in front of the mirror, smile at myself, and put my right hand on the mirror near my face. She wanted to take photos of me doing this action.

So, I did. There I was, wearing a fancy dress, a crown on my pretty hairdo, smiling at myself in the mirror. For the first time in my entire 60 years of life, I thought to myself, "Wow. I'm beautiful!" I shocked myself!

Immediately, God spoke, "Michele, remember years ago when you looked at yourself in the mirror and cursed yourself?"

I then recalled a memory of when in my 20s. I had been so upset one day that I glared at myself in a mirror with eyes of disgust and blurted, "I hate you! I wish you were dead!"

I had since asked the Lord to forgive me for saying that, but the Lord brought it to my mind again.

God continued, "This is a full circle moment for you. Think of that moment years ago, and this moment right now. You finally recognize your beauty and the beauty of my glory within you. I have been patiently waiting for this very moment when you would finally see what I see."

I started to weep.

I then told Nancy what had just happened, then she started to cry. She then shouted, "Michele! God just gave you a key! Do you know what key he gave you?"

She then ran inside and came back to hand me a golden key. She said, "God just gave you the key to extravagantly love yourself! Now you can help others do the same!"

Since that moment, I have never been the same. Something shifted deep within me. I understood and received my worth more fully than ever before. I also realized my love for others expanded and deepened!

There is a glory of God so brilliant, so unique, and so profound shining within you as well!

A few weeks later, my husband commented on how I had significantly changed since the retreat. He shared that I now displayed a greater confidence and sense of security than ever before. Praise King Jesus! Of course, I am still a work in progress!

There is a glory of God so brilliant, so unique, and so profound shining within you as well! Do you see it? Do you love yourself?

I encourage you to try this activity: Every day for a month, journal one thing you love about yourself and write a sentence describing how that one thing expresses something about who God is. Ask the Lord to help you. If you are ambitious, write 100 things you love about yourself over time!

Stepping Stone 4: Discover and Appreciate Your Design

You've probably already taken a number of personality tests and spiritual gift inventories, and you may even be administering them to others. You are like a shining diamond with numerous, unique facets to who you are that reflect aspects of God that only you can reflect.

Knowing your design can help you:

- Refrain from comparing yourself to others.
- Appreciate how God created you.
- Focus on developing your strengths.
- Stir up and use your gifts.
- Establish healthy boundaries.
- Grow in wisdom on what to say yes or no to.
- Increase your fruitfulness, joy, and zest for life!

God has given you specific gifts for you to use to influence the world for good!

God has given you specific gifts for you to use to influence the world for good (see Proverbs 18:16)! How do you like to express yourself? Do you like to express yourself through:

- Writing (poetry, journaling, songwriting, scripts, etc.)
- Painting or sketching
- Making something (woodworking, crafting, cooking, baking, etc.)
- Gardening or home decorating
- Dancing
- Playing an instrument
- Singing
- Dramatic arts
- Photography
- Organizing
- Storytelling or teaching
- Humor
- Other: _____

Knowing your design can also help you know what kinds of activities build you up. Make time to do what fills you so you can be more joyful and successful in all that you do! What do you enjoy doing? What brings you a sense of joy and fun when you do it? What energizes you?

Celebrate your design and the unique design of others around you!

Stepping Stone 5: Dream Big with God

So much of our walk with the Lord is obeying him and following his lead – and rightly so!

In addition, I want to propose that as we follow the Lord, he also wants us to learn how to dream with him. Instead of only working *for* God, we work *with* him.

True story: King David in the Bible had a dream to build God's temple. This was not God's idea – it was David's. At the temple's dedication service, King Solomon shared that the temple originated in the heart of his father David.

God says in Psalm 37:4 that he will give us the desires of our hearts. *Why dream?* You were designed to dream. Our God is a wild, passionate, bold dreamer, and visionary! We were created in his image.

Dreaming also involves activating our God-given creativity and imagination. We need creative solutions and creative wisdom in our daily lives. Creativity involves the arts but is not limited to the arts.

God is the most creative being ever – just look at all the plants and animals! I repeat, you are created in *his* image, which means *you are* creative. Because you are *his* child, you also have access to God's unlimited creativity!

Why Dream? Your dreams can point to your purpose. You were created with great intention. What moves your heart deeply will most probably be part of your life's mission and calling. God wants us to be intentional in walking towards doing what we were designed to do. You were purposed to be a part of something that is meaningful and bigger than yourself.

Why dream? Your dreams could change the world and impact the lives around you in a big way! Picture the possibilities that can lie within a dream. An entire nation was changed under Abraham Lincoln's dream to become president. Every invention was dreamed up by an inventor!

Imagine if you could be part of establishing a dream culture in your organization where everyone encouraged each other to be creative and dream *big* dreams that bring God glory. How would it feel to not only have someone believe in you and your dreams but also have others work alongside you to help those dreams come true? Such a culture would be heavenly!

God purposely planted dreams within you, and he can resurrect dreams that you thought were long gone.

Help Raise, Restore, and Release Others!

In my adventure with God, I have discovered that he is full of surprises. His love is so great for every person in the world. As a missionary who cares for others, God has given you his heart of love for the nations and your colleagues. May these stepping stones remind you to care for yourself even as you care for others *so that* you can help raise, restore, and release others into the glorious fullness of all God offers!

> *"I pray that your hearts will be flooded with light so that you can understand the confident hope he has given to those he called – his holy people who are his rich and glorious inheritance."* (Ephesians 1:18, NLT)

MICHELE OKIMURA is the director of Releasing Generations (explicit-movement.org), an organization which includes three facets: Explicit Movement, Kingdom Families, and ReThink Creativity. Michele and her husband, Rob, served as pastors of Lifespring Church in Honolulu, Hawaii and have two children. Prior to being a pastor, she worked for 17 years as an elementary school teacher.

Questions for Reflection

- What questions in stepping stone 1 were most difficult to answer? What makes them challenging and why?
- Referring to the list of affirming statements under stepping stone 2, were there any statements you had difficulty believing? If so, which statements did you have trouble with and why?
- On a scale of 1–10, (with 10 being you love yourself fully as God wants you to, and 1 being you struggle with loving yourself) what number reflects where you are now? Why that number?
- You have a unique design reflected in how you enjoy expressing yourself. What activity brings you a sense of joy and fills you up? When was the last time you did that activity?
- What are your dreams, and how are you cultivating them?

Additional Resources

Explicit Movement. *The Birth of Explicit Movement: Discover Keys to Fulfilling Your Purpose*. https://explicitmovement.org.

Explicit Movement. *Brave & Beautiful*, 4-Volume Journey Book Sets. Releasing Generations, 2022. https://www.braveandbeautiful.world.

Explicit Movement. *Dream Big Journal: Keys to Unlock Your Dreams*. https://www.explicitmovement.org.

CHAPTER 8

The Family Readiness Discussion

By Faith De La Cour

"LEAVING RIGHT IS A KEY to entering right."[1]

During a couple's final pre-field training week at the SIM USA campus, at least three of us asked a mother if her young adult children would be okay when they left for overseas. Although she had been their primary support until shortly before their departure, she was convinced they would be fine and reluctant to answer more questions.

Within six months of their deployment, they were back in the US. Though each of us had a check in our spirits, we needed a structure in place earlier in our appointee process to communicate our concerns and evaluate the wisdom of our decisions to deploy new staff.

Preliminary Concerns

Within a short time, we had several early exits from overseas service. As a result, the member care team recognized that the

---

1 David C. Pollock, Ruth E. Van Reken, and Michael V. Pollock, *Third Culture Kids: Growing Up Among Worlds, 3rd edition* (Boston: Nicholas Brealey Publishing, 2017), 181.

onboarding process for these global workers was not identifying or responding to family issues in a timely manner. We discovered issues so late in the process that it was hard to pull the plug.

Appointees had already sold their homes, quit their jobs, raised all their financial support, and purchased airline tickets. We held our breath, prayed, and hoped for the best. That usually created unnecessary grief for global workers, their senders, and those who had received them in their ministry location.

As the directors of member care, personnel, and I attended the final candidate screening review, we began to discuss how to screen a family more effectively. We thoroughly screened adults before our acceptance but only saw children after the parents had been appointed to a future ministry location. Our understanding of employment laws has us identify the parents as our future employees, not the children. The screening process we had in place for the children relied on parents' disclosures, not any other assessment.

Once the children accompany parents to campus for pre-field training, our TCK care staff provides an excellent age-appropriate training program for children. Often, this is when concerns relating to the children become evident. They may see children who are not on board with their parents' call to go overseas and feel unheard. There are also times when they become concerned about how parents interact with their children.

At times, problems arise when it is discovered late in the appointee process that children's needs cannot be met in the assigned place of ministry. Possibly, the parents have failed to disclose the child's issues or are unaware of them. After working with the children, the TCK care staff recognized these concerns but sensed that those shepherding the pre-field process needed to be more willing to value their observations and input.

Other family-related matters were also a concern but did not come up in the screening process, such as young adult children and others dependent on the appointee for their well-being. Furthermore, while the *transition process* was taught in-house

The member care team recognized that the onboarding process for these global workers was not identifying or responding to family issues in a timely manner.

and at external preparation programs, it was typically introduced near departure and without sufficient time to put it into practice before leaving.

The Advent of the Family Readiness Discussion

We started to ask, "What would it look like to raise missionary candidates' consciousness on issues of closing well at an earlier point in their journey toward overseas ministry?" Our member care counselor, Clare Hudson, drafted a process[2] to meet with candidates early in their journey toward appointment, which we initially called the *Family Readiness Interview*.

We incorporated the Family Readiness Interview into our in-person, adult-only screening event. Two facilitators would meet in a comfortable setting with the candidates for 30 to 45 minutes. They would prepare a report to share with a review committee.

We broadened our *Readiness Review Committee* to include the TCK Team Leader, who could review the application and references and bring a more well-rounded picture of the applicants and their families. We created a screening rubric modified to a "readiness for overseas ministry" rating. The Family Readiness

---

2 Clare Hudson, "Family Readiness Explanation and Interview Report Form," SIM USA internal document (Charlotte, 2019).

Interview summary was referenced and often matched the screening materials but sometimes provided additional insight and information that would influence the decision of their *readiness*.

Readiness could encompass not only the screening materials, including the psychological assessments, but also observation of the adult and recognition of needs for relational improvements, recommendations for further training or personal development, and, if known, educational or developmental assessments and treatment plans for children. Nevertheless, the timing of this meeting still occurred before the children had come to our campus with their parents.

After several rounds of using the Family Readiness Interview, we concluded that this process was primarily intended for the candidates' benefit, though it occasionally added to screening. To lessen the anxiety that came with the term *interview*, we shifted the name to the *Family Readiness Discussion*.

Coinciding with the onset of the COVID-19 pandemic, the strategy for SIM USA's screening process moved from a four-day in-person event to one done virtually and individually. With that change, the setting for the Family Readiness Discussion moved to zoom. Along with that change came the opportunity to spend more time in the discussion, allowing the candidates to ask questions and brainstorm with the facilitators. While this has worked reasonably well, an in-person discussion is preferred.

Early facilitators included a counselor and a member care facilitator. With time and training, this is now entirely the responsibility of a member care facilitation team, often including a TCK care facilitator. Adding the TCK care facilitator has enriched the conversation with families who have or will have children going with them.

The discussion is relevant for all candidates – singles, families, couples without children or with adult children out of the home. It explores a 360-degree view of the candidate's relationships, from immediate and extended family, work relationships, church responsibilities, and children. It closes with transition tool recommendations. A report is still prepared for the Readiness Review Committee from this discussion, including commendations, suggestions, or concerns to inform those who will coach the candidates if accepted into the appointee process.

Discussion Outline

The conversation opens with the affirmation that the purpose is to guide candidates as they think through the leaving process. They have often not considered the implications of following their call to overseas service on the people within their extended family and community. The following are representative questions and discussion points for each category in this conversation.

PARENTS. Ask if their parents are believers, supportive of missions, and responsive to their intentions to go overseas. Follow up with questions about their relationship with their parents. Do they have concerns about their parent's health? If they are elderly or ill, what plans do they need to have for their care when they go overseas? What responsibilities do they have for their parents, such as being listed as their power of attorney?

SIBLINGS. Ask similar questions regarding siblings. Sometimes a sibling is dependent on the candidate, which initiates a follow-up conversation.

GOODBYES. Considering what they share about their familial connections, the candidate is encouraged to think through how to communicate with them through the mission journey and how to have healthy goodbyes.

MINISTRIES. Inquire about their leadership roles in their local church or other current ministries. Have they thought about transition plans? Could they mentor their successors? Are there natural endpoints for their involvement?

WORK. Ask about their current employment. If they own their own business, what is their plan? Have they told their employer they are considering missions? Can they move to part-time work as they get closer to departure? Consider a conversation about strategies to do this if they still need to.

CHILDREN. The facilitators have a list of the candidate's children and their ages as they ask these questions. Have they talked with their children about their exploration of missionary service? If so, how are they responding? If not, when do they intend to let their children know? How much do they involve their children in these decisions?

Do they have health or developmental concerns for their children? Do they have medical concerns for their children that need to be considered as they look at future placements?

Do any of their children currently have an IEP at school? Having the TCK care facilitator involved in the discussion enables the candidates to explore educational options, hear recommendations for assessments and therapies, and discover the level of commitment our organization has to the well-being of the children they take with them overseas.

Facilitators ask parents if their children have any mentors in their lives. They are encouraged to recognize that there will likely be people in their place of service whom their children will look up to as mentors. Singles and those without children are told about the opportunities and possibly even expectations that they will be mentors to children wherever they will live and serve.

If there is a divorce in the family, whether they are custodial or non-custodial parent will impact their responsibilities and relationships with their children. Whatever the situation, this must be addressed early in the candidate process.

In addition, if the candidates are leaving adult children, we ask about the health and maturity of these family members. Can support people be available to *stand in* when parents are overseas? How do these children feel about their parents moving across the globe?

Since any of these issues figure into the plan for the whole family, we want to be aware of these from the beginning rather than becoming aware later in their appointee process. Bringing them up this early in the process enables the family to think through solutions and responses in a timely manner.

Recommendations

INTENTIONALITY IN GOODBYES. After exploring these various relationships, the discussion moves to resources and strategies that may help the candidates prepare to leave well. They include discussions on staying connected with those who remain in the US and stepping into the emotions of goodbyes.

We challenge them not to ignore their loved ones and friends' pain as the candidates talk about and work toward departing. We ask them to put themselves in the place of these loved ones, mentally consider what they might be thinking, and directly ask their friends and family how they feel about their decision. Know that others are already beginning to feel a loss with them leaving.

The candidate is encouraged to allow friends and family to share their feelings. Can they work together to set up plans to stay in touch, make field visits, and avoid the complicated feelings that come shortly before departure?

Singles are encouraged to converse with anyone they are currently dating regarding their interest in serving overseas. The recommendation is that if they are using dating apps, stop. Frequently questions will come up about dating once on the field, leading to a discussion on the mission's policies.

FORMING A SUPPORT GROUP. We suggest that the candidates gather a small group of friends to pray for them through this journey from acceptance through pre-field preparation, support raising, and on through their arrival and transition to their place of ministry. This intimate support group can be there for them through the thick and thin of their missionary experience. Often, they have not yet thought about this. They are also encouraged to strength-en their relationships and connect with the people responsible for working with them from their sending church.

USING A TRANSITION TOOL. As a closing to the discussion, the fa-cilitators give out a handout with the RAFT exercise –explaining Reconciliation, Affirmation, Farewell, and Transition for good closure. This handout includes definitions of each stage with sample questions to explore how they can apply it to their family. Some families have questioned the importance of having their children say goodbye, hoping to shield them from pain, which provides the TCK care facilitator an opportunity to address the value of this process.

After introducing the RAFT, the facilitator suggests they begin with a *C* to CRAFT an action plan. They receive a sheet where they can begin intentionally praying and listing their 360-degree circle to make a note of who, what, where, and when they need to connect for closure.

C also stands for *celebration* as they see what God has done to bring them to this decision point.

CLOSING. The facilitators let the candidates know they will send a document and follow up on the RAFT exercise and a link to a book, *The Red Sea Rules*,[3] on transition. After asking them for prayer requests, one facilitator will close with prayer. Following the conversation, the facilitators review what they have heard and prepare the report.

The Value of this Discussion

Many participants in this discussion report that it was the most helpful meeting they had so early in the process. It has opened

---

3 Robert J. Morgan, *The Red Sea Rules: 10 God-Given Strategies for Difficult Times* (Nashville: Thomas Nelson, Inc., 2014).

their eyes to the implication that they are not the only ones who will experience change when God calls them to serve overseas. It has encouraged healthy and healing relationships. It has made them aware of the implications of specific placements on their family and helped them choose appropriate locations. They discover how committed SIM USA is to their well-being.

From the organizational perspective, SIM USA Chief Personnel Officer Mark Bosscher wrote, "We are seeing it increasingly as a significant factor in retention, running the gamut from TCK prep to newlywed care to singles needing to work through family-of-origin issues and ongoing care for parents."[4]

Would this discussion have helped the family referenced in the opening? Perhaps so. The hard questions we were asking and that the mother avoided answering would have needed to be addressed and would have been part of the readiness review process. We saw beauty from brokenness as their sending church embraced the family and enabled them to receive the help they needed. They saw their young adult children come to a more stable place and then successfully returned to their original field of ministry after careful rescreening.

FAITH DE LA COUR was a 20-year leader in missionary care, first in Japan with Asian Access, and then as the chief people officer for SIM USA (simusa.org). Recently retired, she champions the need for responsible stewardship of global workers sent by mission organizations and churches. She is a workshop track leader for Missio Nexus and mentors new leaders. Faith has a BS from Wheaton College and an MBA from Northwestern University in organizational behavior.

---

4 Mark Bosscher, email message to author, June 7, 2022.

Questions for Reflection

- How might this discussion be changed for candidates not originally from the US but who have lived here a long time and are preparing to go as missionaries to their *home countries* or another location?
- Adult TCKs wanting to serve, whether in the country of their childhood or another, sometimes assume they do not need to go through the same pre-field processes as non-TCKs. In what ways could this discussion be crafted to encourage them to consider the implications of their decision?

Additional Resources

Morgan, Robert J. *The Red Sea Rules: 10 God-Given Strategies for Difficult Times*. Nashville: Thomas Nelson, Inc., 2014.

CHAPTER 9

Managing Missionary Conflict Constructively

By David R. Dunaetz

ANDREW AND BRANDON HAVE RECENTLY STARTED a pioneer church planting work in a new field with their mission. Andrew thinks that a coffee shop would be the most effective way to meet new people and develop relationships, while also providing a place for future meetings. Brandon believes it is more culturally appropriate to focus on hospitality and visiting people in their homes because sharing meals is the normal context for developing relationships; such an approach also involves much less financial risk. Their disagreement begins to intensify. Will this become a destructive conflict that will hinder their ministries, or could it be constructive and enable greater effectiveness?

Such a situation is very common in missionary contexts when missionaries work closely with each other and are highly dependent on one another, especially if they expect their team to be an important source of emotional support and encouragement. The initial tension can escalate and become destructive, eventually

Originally published in a slightly different form from Dunaetz, D. R. "Missionary Conflict: Destructive or Constructive?" *Evangelical Missions Quarterly* 58, no. 2 (2022): 57–59. Reprinted by permission.

contributing to one or both missionaries leaving the field.[1]

However, if managed correctly, their conflict can be construc-tive, leading to a solution that is better than either of Andrew or Brandon's original ideas. If the missionaries are aware of each other's concerns, their differences of perspective, and any power imbalances that exist within their team, a constructive conflict becomes much more likely. That will enable them to work better as a team making continued ministry more fruitful.

Missionary conflict is inevitable and potentially dangerous if mismanaged. However, when missionaries in conflict seek to cooperate by understanding each other's perspectives and in-terests, creative solutions can be found. This requires time and effort, and sometimes outside help. However, cooperation with a desire to love and serve the other is a Christ-like response that is well worth the cost.

The Dual Concern Model of Interpersonal Relationships

To understand a conflict, it is useful to understand what each party is concerned about, that is, their interests. The dual concern model of conflict management (model simply means a simplifi-cation of a complex reality focusing on only a few key aspects) describes four different ways people respond in conflicts based on the focus of their interests.[2]

---

1 Rob Hay et al., *Worth Keeping: Global Perspectives on Best Practice in Missionary Retention* (Pasadena, CA: William Carey Library, 2007).

2 Ralph H. Kilmann and Kenneth W. Thomas, "Developing a Forced-Choice Measure of Conflict-Handling Behavior: the 'Mode' Instrument," *Educational and Psychological Measurement* 37, no. 2 (1977); David R. Dunaetz, "Submission or Cooperation? Two Competing Approaches to Conflict Management in Mission Organizations," in *Controversies in Mission: Theology, People, and Practice in the 21st Century*, ed. R. Cathcart Scheuermann and E. L. Smither (Pasadena, CA: William Carey Library, 2016); Jeffery Z. Rubin, Dean G. Pruitt, and Sung H. Kim, *Social Conflict: Escalation, Stalemate, and Settlement*, ed. Philip G. Zimbardo,

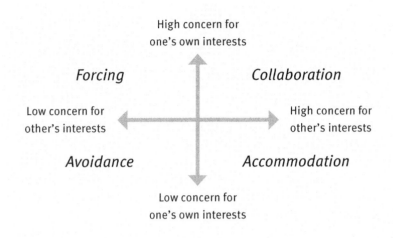

High concern for
one's own interests

Forcing *Collaboration*

Low concern for   High concern for
other's interests   other's interests

Avoidance *Accommodation*

Low concern for
one's own interests

Figure 1. The Dual Concern Model of Conflict.

When Andrew and Brandon are having a conflict, their interests can be divided into two sets: the interests of Andrew and the interests of Brandon. Andrew has four ways to approach the conflict (see figure 1).[3] First, he can be concerned about his interests, but not those of Brandon (high concern for self, low concern for other). In this case, his approach might be characterized by *forcing*, using his power to get Andrew to accept what he wants. A second option is *accommodation* (low concern for self, high concern for other), deciding to only be concerned about Andrew's interests and denying his own.

A third approach is to simply decide that the disagreement is not worth discussing, which leads to *avoidance* (low concern for

2nd ed., McGraw-Hill Series in Social Psychology (New York: McGraw-Hill, 1994).
3 Rubin, Pruitt, and Kim, *Social Conflict*; Dunaetz, "Submission or Cooperation?"; W. W. Wilmot and J. L. Hocker, *Interpersonal Conflict*, 8th ed. (McGraw Hill, 2011).

When missionaries disagree with each other, often both have legitimate concerns.

self, low concern for other). A fourth approach, *collaboration*, describes a situation with both high concern for one's own interests and high concern for the other's interests. If Andrew and Brandon want to collaborate, they will first strive to understand what each other is concerned about and then will consider various solutions that will maximize addressing all these concerns.

This fourth approach (*collaboration*, sometimes called *cooperation*) has been empirically demonstrated to lead to the best outcomes in organizations[4] including mission organizations.[5] Not surprisingly, this is the exact approach that Paul recommended to the church in Philippi, "Let each of you look not only to his own interests, but also to the interest of others" (Philippians 2:4, ESV). When missionaries disagree with each other, often both have legitimate concerns. Solutions that address all of these concerns are the best, but they often demand much time, effort, and creativity to find.

Missionary Conflict Should Be Expected

Mission organizations generally have a clear purpose specific to

---

4 Jonathan A. Rhoades and Peter J. Carnevale, "The Behavioral Context of Strategic Choice in Negotiation: A Test of the Dual Concern Model," *Journal of Applied Social Psychology* 29, no. 9 (1999); M. Afzalur Rahim, *Managing Conflict in Organizations*, 3rd ed. (Westport, CT: Quorum Books, 2001).

5 David R. Dunaetz and Ant Greenham, "Power or Concerns: Contrasting Perspectives on Missionary Conflict," *Missiology: An International Review* 46, no. 1 (2018).

the organization (e.g., fulfilling the Great Commission or demonstrating God's love through economic development). But how this purpose plays out in a specific context may be anything but clear. Missionaries working in teams must coordinate their efforts if they wish to accomplish anything. They need to share a common vision, a common set of values, and a common strategy. However, missionaries often come from vastly different backgrounds.

Andrew and Brandon may both love God and his Word, but they also have distinct personalities, perspectives, and knowledge. Andrew is more extroverted and previously worked in the restaurant industry. He can't imagine a better form of outreach than a coffee shop. Brandon is quieter and has led several of his close, long-term friends to Christ in their homes. He can't picture himself in a coffee shop ministry. Because their different backgrounds prevent them from understanding each other, the tension in their relationship escalates.

Our different backgrounds shape the lenses through which we view the world. Andrew and Brandon both see opportunities for ministry through their own uniquely shaped lens. This creates the foundation for conflicts. To cooperate, Andrew and Brandon need to understand one another's lens so that they see the situation from the other's point of view. This enables them to consider each other's interests and concerns. However, understanding another's perspective requires hard work.

Collaboration is Difficult

From a scriptural point of view, collaboration seems like it would be a natural first choice since this approach aligns nicely with the concepts of love, service, and humility. However, it can take a lot of time and effort, requiring more than what Andrew or Brandon may be ready to provide. This is especially true if there is a power imbalance, that is, one missionary has more power than the other.

For example, if Brandon is the field chair, he may have the

authority to tell Andrew what they are going to do. This requires far less effort than coming up with a solution that addresses both his and Andrew's concerns. Such an approach is forcing, or "lording it over" (Matthew 20:25–26), which is the opposite of serving the other.

Forcing one's will on the other is fast, efficient, and, perhaps in some rare cases, could be considered an appropriate last resort, but it will damage the relationship, perhaps permanently, and prevent a potentially better solution from emerging.[6] A ministry with a leader who uses such tactics is not likely to be very fruitful, at least from God's perspective (1 Peter 5:2–3; cf. Demetrius in 3 John 9–11).

An imbalance of power may also occur if one missionary is more verbally fluent and can process information more quickly than the other. If Andrew presents many reasons for his ideas faster than Brandon can understand them, Andrew may come across as trying to deceive or trick Brandon. In this case, Andrew needs to be careful not to force more information on Brandon quicker than Brandon can handle it. This makes cooperation even more difficult and time demanding.

If Brandon has positional power but Andrew has the power that comes from fluency, it is quite possible that Brandon will use his power to avoid addressing the issues that concern Andrew, or, in the worst-case scenario, use his power to remove Andrew from ministry. Andrew needs to learn how to slow down and work on persuading Brandon of the validity of his concerns in a way that does not threaten Brandon. Nevertheless, in some cases, an outside mediator will be necessary. Wise mission organization leaders will provide such a structure and encourage missionaries to use it.[7]

6 Dunaetz and Greenham, "Power or Concerns"; Dunaetz, "Submission or Cooperation?"

7 David R. Dunaetz, "Long Distance Managerial Intervention in Overseas Conflicts: Helping Missionaries Reframe Conflict Along Multiple Dimensions,"

A mediator can come
alongside two missionaries
in conflict and help them find
a solution that they both find
satisfactory and beneficial.

Mediation

Sometimes understanding each other's perspective and interests is so difficult that it requires outside help from a third party. A mediator can come alongside two missionaries in conflict and help them find a solution that they both find satisfactory and beneficial. In general, mediation is a very effective way to resolve conflict.[8] Not only can it lead to a constructive solution that benefits both missionaries, but it can make their relationship stronger as they understand each other better and grow in mutual trust.

Who Should be the Mediator?

Mediation is different than both adjudication and arbitration.[9] In adjudication, a judge has the legal power to choose the outcome

Missiology: An International Review 38, no. 3 (2010).

8 P. J. Carnevale and D. G. Pruitt, "Negotiation and Mediation," *Annual Review of Psychology* 43, no. 1 (1992): 531–582; D. G. Pruitt and P. J. Carnevale, *Negotiation in Social Conflict* (Thomson Brooks/Cole Publishing Co., 1993).

9 Wilmot and Hocker, *Interpersonal Conflict.*

after hearing each party's evidence and argument. In arbitration, this power is given to an expert who understands the technicalities involved and is committed to fairness. However, in mediation, the mediator simply helps the two parties come up with a solution that is acceptable to both. The two parties are not adversaries, but rather collaborators who work together in a process directed by the mediator.

This means that the mediator must be impartial and trusted by both missionaries. If the mediator is not impartial or trusted by both parties, collaboration is less likely. One missionary can quickly feel that the mediator is more aligned with the other missionary, which may hinder the communication needed for constructive problem-solving.

In missionary contexts, location and culture become important factors in determining who should be a mediator. Ideally, the mediator should be someone who can physically meet with both of the missionaries to make effective communication more likely. This might mean that the missionaries ask a trusted member of the local culture or a coworker from their home culture whom they both trust to be a mediator.

However, such a person might not exist. In that case, meeting with a trusted person from their sending organization via video conferencing might be appropriate. To be an effective mediator, this person should be known by both missionaries, either personally or through endorsement by mission organization leaders who have encouraged the use of a mediator.

Sometimes mission organizations have a designated mediator (or ombudsman) who is a member of the organization or who has a contract with the organization to help out when a mediator is needed. For mediation to be effective, both missionaries must trust this person; if mission organizations promote using this person as a mediator before conflicts occur, missionaries are more likely to trust him or her, increasing the likelihood of successful conflict resolution.

The Mediation Process

There is no *right* way to do mediation. Any process which will get the missionaries to collaborate constructively to resolve their conflict is appropriate. However, there are some general steps that many mediators follow. These include initial meetings with the two parties separately, one or more problem-solving sessions, and follow-up.

INITIAL INDIVIDUAL MEETINGS. If Andrew and Brandon agree to mediation, and if they both trust Charles who is willing to play the role of the mediator, Charles may meet with each missionary separately to clarify what is going on and what the issues are. Charles will ask Andrew probing questions to understand why a coffee shop ministry is so important to him and what he expects the outcomes to be.

Charles will ask about other concerns that Andrew has. Those concerns are often more psychological such as how the coffee shop ministry relates to his identity, what he wants his relationship with Brandon to look like, and what he considers a fair way to resolve the conflict.[10] Charles will also explain that the purpose of the mediation process is to help Andrew and Brandon to work together to find a mutually beneficial solution to their conflict.

He will ask Andrew if he agrees to that purpose and if he is willing to follow some basic ground rules requiring a willingness

---

10 For a detailed explanation of what these concerns might look like in missionary contexts and why they are important, see: D.R. Dunaetz, "Mission in Evolving Cultures: Constructively Managing Music-related Conflict in Cross-cultural Church Planting Contexts," *Missiology: An International Review* 44, no. 3 (2016): 296–310; D. R. Dunaetz, "Constructively Managing Program-related Conflict in Local Churches," *Christian Education Journal* 16, no. 2 (2019): 259–274.

to listen to Brandon's point of view and to speak only in a respect-ful way when they all meet together. After meeting with Andrew, Charles will organize a similar meeting with Brandon.

MEETING ALL TOGETHER. After connecting with the two missionaries individually, the mediator (Charles) will organize a meeting for all three of them together. At this meeting, Charles will again emphasize that the purpose of the meeting is so that Andrew and Brandon can figure out a solution together that responds to both the concerns of both. He will also explain the importance of the ground rules concerning respect and listening to each other.

After gaining verbal agreement to the process, Charles will ask one of the missionaries to explain what he wants first, and then ask the other to share what he wants. Charles will guide the con-versation so that Andrew expresses all the concerns that he had previously shared with Charles, making sure that Brandon can provide feedback to Andrew demonstrating that either he under-stands these concerns or that he needs additional information to understand them. Similarly, Charles makes sure Brandon shares all his concerns and that Andrew understands them.

After all the concerns have been clearly communicated, Charles will lead the two missionaries into a period of brainstorming of possible solutions. The possible solutions will be discussed, evaluated, and possibly modified. An important part of this dis-cussion is negotiation, modifying a proposal so that a maximum number of interests are met in a mutually beneficial way.[11] Some Christians confuse negotiation with moral compromise and thus refuse to modify their initial proposal or demands. The role of the mediator is to make clear that most, if not all, of what is being

---

11 C. K. W. de Dreu, S. L. Koole, W. Steinel, "Unfixing the Fixed Pie: A Motivated Information-processing Approach to Integrative Negotiation," *Journal of Personality and Social Psychology* 79, no. 6 (2000): 975–987; Wilmot and Hocker, *Interpersonal Conflict*.

Some Christians confuse negotiation with moral compromise and thus refuse to modify their initial proposal or demands.

negotiated is not a question of moral right or wrong.[12] In this case, there are no biblical injunctions against either witnessing in a coffee house or in individuals' homes.

Charles will ensure that Andrew and Brandon keep negotiating until they come to a mutually beneficial solution. In this case, Andrew and Brandon agree to set up a coffee shop for an initial six-month trial. They will measure the success of the coffee shop ministry by the number of visits made to the homes of the people whom they had met in the coffee shop.

Andrew and Brandon tentatively agree that if during the first six months, they each visit at least 20 families because of this ministry, it will be a success. This solution responds to both Andrew's concern for starting a coffee shop ministry and Brandon's concerns of limiting the financial risk and focusing on meeting in people's homes.

FOLLOW UP. To close the negotiating session or sessions, Charles will encourage Andrew and Brandon to write down their agreement. After several months, Charles may contact them to see how it is going. It is possible that further mediation might be necessary, especially if the trial solution is not going well. But it is even more likely that Andrew and Brandon have learned, through this process, how to constructively manage their disagreements.

---

12 L. Greenhalgh, "Managing Conflict," *Sloan Management Review* 27, no. 4 (1986): 45–52.

Recommendations

Although collaboration ought to be the default approach to managing conflict on a missionary team, finding possible solutions that take into consideration each missionary's perspective, values, interests, and concerns is time-consuming, hard work. Philippians 2:4 describes collaboration perfectly, "Let each of you look not only to his own interests, but also to the interests of others" (ESV). The preceding verse explains how we can do it: "Do nothing from selfish ambition or conceit, but in humility count others more significant than yourselves" (Philippians 2:3, ESV). The verses which follow underscore that such collaboration is a manifestation of the Christlikeness to which we as Christians and as missionaries are called, "Have this mind among yourselves which is yours in Christ Jesus, who ... emptied himself, by taking the form of a servant" (Philippians 2:5–7a).

DAVID R. DUNAETZ is chair and professor of leadership, organizational psychology, and public administration at Azusa Pacific University, in California (apu.edu). He previously served as a church planting missionary for 17 years with WorldVenture in France.

Questions for Reflection

- This chapter presents collaboration as the best solution to missionary conflict in most situations. What do you think are some of the greatest barriers to collaboration? What can be done to reduce these barriers?
- Occasionally, forcing, accommodation, or avoiding might be better responses to missionary conflict than collaboration. Under what conditions might each of these be the most appropriate response?

CHAPTER 10

Supervisory Relationships and Well-Being

By Kimberly Drage and Hyon Kim

LIMITING OUR UNDERSTANDING OF CARE for global workers to individual services and training, limits our capacity to provide effective care. As we look at the world of work broadly, very few organizations provide *on-site* counseling and care services. And yet, many of these same organizations are committed to the well-being of their people. How? One of the primary ways they do this is by aiming to understand how the organization, itself, influences well-being.

As we have pursued well-being within the world of missions, the majority of our attention has been focused at an individual level with an emphasis on activities such as candidate screening, individual care services, and training in cross-cultural resilience. The clear importance of individual-level care makes it no less incomplete as we consider how best to support global workers.

Thankfully, this gap is being acknowledged. The collective responsibility and influence of organizations on well-being continues to emerge as a topic in member care conversations. This is evidenced by the April 2022 edition of *Evangelical Missions Quarterly* (*EMQ*) devoted specifically to member care. This issue includes an article focused on organizational commitment and culture[1] as well as findings from the "Resilient Global Worker" (RGW) study. RGW focused on ways organizations can support resilience for global workers.[2]

I (Hyon) also recently published an article addressing burnout for global workers which highlights the World Health Organization's definition of burnout, not as an individual condition, but an *occupational phenomenon*. As I shared in the article, "The definition recognizes that burnout is not solely about an individual's resources or coping strategies. Rather, burnout can be prevented and managed by focusing on protective and contributing systemic factors in the workplace."[3]

My (Kimberly's) own research – the "Role of Organizations in Missionary Well-Being" (ROMWB) study – points out many ways organizations influence well-being that go beyond traditional member care. One area that stood out was the influential role of immediate supervisors.[4] This is echoed in broader organizational research on well-being in the workplace.

Supervisory Relationships and Well-being in Organizational Research

Research in the management, organizational psychology and occupational health literature points to a clear connection between well-being at work and immediate supervision. This relationship is related to a variety of health and well-being outcomes

1 Wendi Dykes McGehee, "Do Your Members Really Want to Work for You?" *Evangelical Missions Quarterly* 58, no. 2 (April 2022): 33–35.

2 Geoff Whiteman and Kristina Whiteman, "Supporting Today's Global Workers Toward Missional Resilience," *Evangelical Missions Quarterly* 58, no. 2 (April 2022): 27–29.

3 Hyon Kim, "Caring for Global Mission Workers – Burning Out Burnout," *Asian Mission Advance* 29, no. 3 (Summer 2022): 1–6.

4 Kimberly Drage, "The Role of Mission Organizations in Missionary Well-Being," *Evangelical Missions Quarterly* 57, no. 3 (July 2021): 26–29.

Research in the management, organizational psychology and occupational health literature points to a clear connection between well-being at work and immediate supervision.

including stress levels, heart health, sleep, anxiety, depression, and burnout.[5]

One review in the field of occupational health identifies this influence on well-being as the result of leaders modeling healthy or unhealthy work behaviors, leaders' capacity to respond to one's work positively or negatively, and the power leaders have to shape work so that it is more or less stressful.[6]

Another review found a possible connection between higher stress levels in immediate supervisors and poorer well-being among those they serve. This same review found that quality relationships with supervisors as well as supportive experiences and taking worker's perspectives into consideration led to increased well-being and lower stress for their subordinates.[7]

The implications of this research point to the importance of

---

5 Cynthia D. Fisher, "Happiness at Work," *International Journal of Management Reviews* 12, no. 4 (2010): 384–412, https://doi.org/10.1111/j.1468-2370.2009.00270.x. See additional resources for more on well-being outcomes.

6 Kelloway and Barling, "Leadership Development," 260–79.

7 Janne Skakon, Karina Nielsen, Vilhelm Borg, and Jaime Guzman, "Are Leaders' Well-Being, Behaviours and Style Associated with the Affective Well-Being of Their Employees? A Systematic Review of Three Decades of Research," *Work & Stress* 24, no. 2 (April 1, 2010): 107–39, https://doi.org/10.1080/02678373.2010.495262.

caring for and supporting this essential relationship as well as the potential to improve well-being through the development of both skilled and holistically healthy supervisors.[8] As Gilbreath and Benson comment, "… supervisor behavior *can* affect employee well-being and suggests that those seeking to create healthier workplaces should not neglect supervision"[9] (italics added).

Supervisory Relationships and Well-Being in Missions Research

One key theme emerged from the ROMWB study: the contrast in well-being when global workers experienced connection and disconnection from their organizations. In general, when organizations found effective ways to connect with the needs and aims of global workers and respond in relevant ways, well-being improved.

Conversely, when organizations operated in ways that were perceived as disconnected from (frustrating or even hindering) the needs or aims of global workers, well-being diminished.[10] This theme provides a lens for us to consider the missions research related to immediate supervisors. It is important to note that little published research on immediate supervisors within missions exists. More is needed.[11]

---

8 Brad Gilbreath and Philip G. Benson, "The Contribution of Supervisor Behaviour to Employee Psychological Well-Being," Work & Stress 18, no. 3 (July 1, 2004): 255–66, https://doi.org/10.1080/02678370412331317499. Kelloway and Barling, "Leadership Development," 260–79. Jaana Kuoppala, Anne Lamminpää, Juha Liira, and Harri Vainio. "Leadership, Job Well-Being, and Health Effects – A Systematic Review and a Meta-Analysis," *Journal of Occupational and Environmental Medicine* 50, no. 8 (2008): 904–15.

9 Gilbreath and Benson, "The Contribution," 255.

10 Drage, "The Role of Mission Organizations," 26–29.

11 I (Kimberly) have done my best to gather the available research and will also be including findings from the "Role of Organizations in Missionary Well-Being"

DISCONNECTED SUPERVISORY RELATIONSHIPS. Evidence from missions research indicates that disconnected supervisory relationships can diminish global worker well-being. These disconnected relationships take the form of supervisory absence, incompetence, and abuse, all of which have implications for global worker well-being. As Bessel van der Kolk asserts, "… Trauma almost invariably involves not being seen, not being mirrored, and not being taken into account."[12]

DISCONNECTION THROUGH ABSENCE. Absence is a key theme when it comes to immediate supervision and well-being in missions. Julie Irvine and her colleagues studied traumatic stress in missions. They found that failure of organizational support relationships, including supervisory relationships, was the most common form of traumatic stress reported with the longest lasting negative impact for global workers. This is noteworthy, as we might expect crisis experiences to be the most significant sources of traumatic stress for global workers.[13]

While passive leadership styles can be found in all types of workplaces, there were key insights specific to missions that emerged from my research. The first is that, due to the remote nature of our work and our organizational structures, immediate supervisors can be one of the only consistent links a person has to the organization. If this person is absent or unavailable, it can have a huge impact.

One participant suffered deeply as a result of being almost entirely cut off from organizational support. This occurred during

---

that have not yet been published.

12 Bessel van der Kolk, *The Body Keeps the Score: Mind, Brain and Body in the Transformation of Trauma* (Great Britain: Penguin Books, 2014), 68.

13 Julie Irvine, David P. Armentrout, and Linda A. Miner, "Traumatic Stress in a Missionary Population: Dimensions and Impact," *Journal of Psychology and Theology* 34, no. 4 (December 1, 2006): 327–36, https://doi.org/10.1177/009164710603400403.

Evidence from missions research indicates that disconnected supervisory relationships can diminish global worker well-being.

an extended period of leadership transition that left her without an immediate supervisor. In her context immediate supervisors were the gatekeepers to most organizational resources.

Second, planned leadership absence is quite common within mission organizations both for *home assignment* as well as leadership transition. When these positions go unfilled or temporarily filled with unsupported leaders, there can be considerable implications for the well-being for global workers.[14]

Leader absence was also documented in Ant Greenham's work[15] and in the RGW study. In fact, *negligent leadership* was the most common criticism of leadership documented in that study.[16]

DISCONNECTION DUE TO INCOMPETENCE. Missions research also shows instances of supervisors trying to do well in their roles, but their attempts fail to meet the needs or support the aims of global workers. The RGW study found examples of leaders failing to clarify roles and expectations or struggling with management of the resources or responsibilities in their care.[17]

---

14 Drage, "The Role of Mission Organizations," 26–29.

15 Ant Greenham, "Power Encounter – of the Wrong Kind: A Preliminary Phenomenological Survey on Inappropriate Exercise of Power Experienced by Short-Term Missionaries," *Occasional Bulletin of the Evangelical Mission Society* 29, no. 1 (2016): 1, 3–7, 22.

16 Whiteman and Whiteman, "Supporting Today's Global Workers," 27–29.

17 Whiteman and Whiteman, "Supporting Today's Global Workers," 27–29.

In the ROMWB study, this incompetence was also expressed in the inability to handle team conflict and a lack of substantive help when meeting with supervisees. As one participant reflected, "I would share things with him, but there was no practical help from his side, besides maybe some words of encouragement or some general ideas. But at no point did I feel my interaction with him helped lighten the load at all." This under-supported temporary leader ended up leaving the field in burnout.[18]

The inadequacy of his leadership was part of what contributed to his own diminishing well-being. Of course, this means all the people under his care were also experiencing leader incompetence and absence, which likely had implications for their well-being as well.[19]

WHEN DISCONNECTION BECOMES VIOLATION. It is important to address the very real possibility of abuse within supervisory relationships. This is true within all workplaces, but particular vulnerabilities are present when abuse takes place within missions. For global workers, work touches on almost every other aspect of life including where you live as well as your spirituality. These factors can amplify the power of immediate supervisors as the implications of their decisions and narratives can be so great.

Ant Greenham's research found numerous abuses of supervisory power within missions including making changes to work or freedom without consulting global workers and stifling global worker's voices, at times using spiritual narratives to do so. As one respondent shared, "those who were quiet and reserved were

---

18 The Engage! study found that 7/10 people came to the field not realizing they would be put in a management position. Those who stayed on the field "were more than twice as likely to have received specific training for their leadership role," James Nelson, "The Engage! Study Executive Summary," Missio Nexus (2010), https://missionexus.org/the-engage-study-executive-summary/.

19 Drage, "The Role of Mission Organizations," 26–29.

said to be *humble* and those who questioned the systems were *prideful*."[20]

Spiritual abuse was also evident in the RGW study along with a number of other unjust or immoral behaviors which were categorized as *corrupt leadership*. There was also indication that some leaders in this group were struggling with their own mental health issues or burnout.[21] This points to the possibility that supporting the well-being of immediate supervisors could be one way to avoid disconnection in supervisory relationships.

Connected Supervisory Relationships

While there is even less mission-specific research on what can go right (as opposed to what can go wrong) in supervisory relationships,[22] there are still important insights available to us.

CONNECTION THROUGH PRESENCE. Presence, both emotional and simply time together, emerged in the ROMWB study as one way in which immediate supervisors contributed to well-being. These relationships were often marked by rhythms of regular meetings and being present to the highs and lows of these global workers' experiences.

In some cases, supervisors were readily identified as friends. Presence helped supervisors to see global workers and respond to their needs in relevant ways.[23] Christoper Rosik studied the long-term effects of a high-intensity mental health intervention for Christian ministers. He found that a small number of global

---

20 Greenham, "Power Encounter," 5.

21 Whiteman and Whiteman, "Supporting Today's Global Workers," 27–29.

22 In *the Resilient Global Worker Study* only six people had positive comments to share when engaging the topic of leadership compared to 96 who shared something negative.

23 Kimberly Drage, unpublished research findings from "The Role of Mission Organizations in Missionary Well-Being."

It is important to address the very real possibility of abuse within supervisory relationships.

workers were supported in their healing journey by leadership that listened and made adjustments to their job in response to their needs.[24]

Supportive presence looked different for different people. For example, one person expressed appreciation for the *hands-off* approach of his supervisor which allowed him space to do ministry. Though the supervisor was not directive in his approach, he regularly checked in and made himself available when needed.[25]

CONNECTION THROUGH DEVELOPMENT. Empowerment was another way immediate supervisors increased the well-being of global workers. This took several forms beginning with a genuine desire to see workers grow (both professionally and spiritually). Other forms of empowerment included:

- Providing opportunities for trying new things marked by both freedom and feedback
- Walking alongside global workers through seeking God's guidance
- Work accountability
- Encouragement to go beyond their comfort zones
- Help setting reasonable expectations for themselves

---

24 Christopher H. Rosik, "Long-Term Outcomes of an Intensive Outpatient Program for Missionaries and Clergy," *Journal of Psychology and Christianity* 30, no. 3 (2011).

25 Drage, "The Role of Mission Organizations."

As one participant commented, "You know, I don't know how else to explain it, except that they really walked alongside me, ... comforted me when I needed comfort, and pushed me when I needed pushing."[26]

Bringing Research to Our Practice

The case for the impact immediate supervisors have on the well-being of global workers is compelling, but what does this mean for our organizations?

Reflections & Experience from Mission Leadership

As we discuss the role of supervisory relationships in the well-being of global workers, the story in Genesis 16 of Hagar provides an opportunity for deeper reflection. In this story Hagar, who is pregnant, becomes embroiled in a painful conflict with her mistress, Sarai.

In deep distress, Hagar runs away and is met by the Lord who calls out to her, "Hagar, slave of Sarai, where have you come from, and where are you going?" (Genesis 16:8, NIV). As their conversation unfolds Hagar is instructed to return to her mistress and told that she would have a son. In response, Hagar exclaims, "You are the God who sees me .... I have now seen the One who sees me" (Genesis 16:13, NIV).

What can we learn from Hagar's joy at seeing the God who saw her? What was the nature of God's *seeing* that met such an important need in Hagar? In my mission experience, I (Hyon) have been blessed and inspired by examples of flourishing supervisory relationships. Unfortunately, I have also witnessed the anguish of distressed individuals who felt their supervisors were difficult, disengaged, or uncaring.

One global worker, who spent decades in a remote village

---

26 Drage, "The Role of Mission Organizations."

involved in evangelism and discipleship pulled, me aside and tearfully shared, "In all these years, my supervisor never visited me ... not once!" This worker deeply desired to be seen by his supervisor. A visit would have communicated that he was valued and cared for. But this kind of *seeing* did not happen, or at least not in the way that this worker had expected.

Unlike a disengaged supervisor, God does not simply make note of Hagar's dilemma and move on with the task of fulfilling his promise to Abram. Similarly global workers are not resources on par with monetary or proprietary assets sent out to fulfill a defined ministry purpose. It seems unfathomable for any mission organization or its leaders supporting such a notion.

However, sometimes our organizational policies, practices, and supervisory relationships inadvertently communicate to workers that they are just that – a means to an end. One way to counter this is to help immediate supervisors see the role of supervision as an essential ministry. Help them see their role as part of a broader vision to see that every person who comes through the organization is supported to grow more like Jesus.

In the Hagar story, God's *seeing* is not simply about monitoring or evaluation. While some workers describe their supervisors as uninvolved and disinterested, their same supervisors may feel that they care deeply as they enumerate a worker's strategic ministry activities. In such cases it's not that supervisors don't get involved, but they don't do it in a way that yields a sense of connection. Instead, their involvement communicates to the worker that monitoring and evaluating ministries for alignment with organizational goals is their main priority.

Encouraging regular supervisory engagement and development of relationships prior to a worker's annual review is an important step. In this way, the review can be received as a joyful opportunity to reflect on God's past activities and discern his leading for future ministry strategies in the context of an ongoing supportive relationship.

So how can the supervisory relationship flourish and what

Sometimes our organizational policies, practices, and supervisory relationships inadvertently communicate to workers that they are just … a means to an end.

more can we learn from this story?

FIRSTLY, GOD SHOWS UP. God comes close to Hagar and engages with her and the problem she is experiencing. In the same way, how often and in what ways are supervisors in our organizations engaged with their workers?

There are amazing examples of leaders making it a priority to be physically present with their workers, to spend time with them and understand their contexts. *Showing up* can be a costly commitment, but organizations can support these relationships by prioritizing the allocation of funds for supervisors to travel and for workers to meet at team retreats.

SECONDLY, GOD KNOWS. God calls Hagar by her name and knows that she works as the slave of Sarai. This is not a small detail, but deeply significant as it communicates to Hagar that she is not mere chattel, but a person with a name and identity who exists in the context of an important relationship (albeit dysfunctional).

How much interest do we show in our workers as people: their gifts, passions, and the relationships and communities they are involved in? Supervisors who take as much interest in work as in the updates about family whose well-being figures largely in each person's ability to carry out their current role, demonstrate real care.

THIRDLY, GOD ENGAGES. God asks Hagar, "… where have you come from, and where are you going?" (Genesis 16:8, NIV). What a great coaching question. Even though God is all knowing, he asks Hagar an open-ended question and gives her a voice. This kind of curiosity communicates care and opens the door for greater connectedness.

One of the most encouraging questions anyone can ask is *what do you think*? And when that kind of question comes from a supervisor, it moves from encouraging to thrilling. It is thrilling to have a supervisor who adopts a learner's attitude, genuinely seeks opinions from their team and acknowledges the value of contributions. This is an important stepping-stone towards connection and authentic relationships.

FOURTHLY, GOD LISTENS. God's listening is closely linked to his caring and in turn his actions. After Hagar explains her situation, God tells her to return to her mistress, but does so with her dignity restored as she is assured by God that he has heard her misery. God listened and responded to the deepest need of her heart. How well do mission organizations train supervisors in the art of active listening?

I (Hyon) learned from my previous work as a palliative care physician, how important it is to listen and to be fully present for my patients. In my current role leading a global team, I apply these principles by building short *corridor* times between my virtual meetings. These are times when I intentionally disengage with my previous activity and collect myself for the coming activity by asking the Lord to help me *see* as he does. It is sobering to remember that those we supervise may wait patiently for days or weeks to speak with us, so they deserve our wholehearted attention.

FINALLY, GOD RECEIVES. In other words, the relationship between Hagar and God was mutual, and recursive. It is mutual in the sense that God allows Hagar the privilege of blessing him with a name. "You are the God who sees me..." (Genesis 16:13, NIV). A supervisor's ability to be a gracious receiver requires an element of vulnerability as they reveal a need which another is allowed to meet.

There is also a recursive element in their relationship when Hagar exclaims "I have now seen the One who sees me" (Genesis 16:13, NIV). It is the back and forth knowing that people experience when authentic connection is experienced. It is what allows people to say, "I see you – I see you seeing me – I see you seeing that I see you – I see what you see – I see that you see what I see – I see that you see that I see you seeing that which you see."[27]

God's involvement or *seeing* was a deeply relational interaction that met a fundamental need in Hagar's heart for connectedness. And while we can draw on many relationships to meet such needs, there is something unique about the supervisory relationship, where one person is given a high trust to shepherd, serve and steward another person that requires intentional effort and careful study.[28] It is no less than the call Jesus gave to Peter, "Do you love me .... Feed my lambs ... take care of my sheep ... Feed my sheep" (John 21, NIV). I (Hyon) want to get better at this – how about you?

Conclusion

As we continue journeying together in supporting the well-being of global workers, we must look beyond a direct services approach to care. As we turn our attention toward the organizational responsibilities connected to care, the role of immediate supervisors is one key area that comes into focus. As we consider this key role,

27 B. Siposova and M. Carpenter, "A New Look at Joint Attention and Common Knowledge," *Cognition* 189 (August 2019): 260–274, https://doi.org/10.1016/j.cognition.2019.03.019.

28 D. Bremner, *Images of Leadership: Biblical Portraits of Godly Leaders* (South Africa: Oasis International Ltd, 2021), 18–44.

A supervisor's ability to be a gracious receiver requires an element of vulnerability as they reveal a need which another is allowed to meet.

may our imaginations be open to the ways we can support global worker well-being by supporting supervisory relationships. Here are some initial ideas:

- Proactively support the well-being of immediate supervisors (ex. supporting spiritual vitality, work-life balance, nourishing relationships and providing them with supervision that empowers their role).
- Affirm supervision as an essential part of ministry and develop a theological and practical foundation to support that work. This could include things such as ongoing training in how to be present and develop (to *see*) those they are supervising or setting clear aims for supervisory relationships.[29]
- Establish regular avenues for feedback to unearth blind spots and absences in supervisory relationships.[30] (This includes

---

29 The "go-to" framework at SIM is the shepherd, steward, servant, and shared leadership models in Scripture developed by Dave Bremner, who is our leadership development lead; Bremner, *Images of Leadership*.

30 Edmondson and Wilder both advocate for the development of organizational cultures of safety to support healthy relationships; Amy C. Edmondson, *The Fearless Organization: Creating Psychological Safety in the Workplace for Learning, Innovation, and Growth* (Wiley, 2018); and James E. Wilder, *The Pandora Problem: Facing Narcissism in Leaders and Ourselves* (Deeper Walk International, 2018).

the very important task of establishing clear policies and procedures for responding to abusive leadership).[31]

This list is neither exhaustive nor prescriptive. It is a starting point for your own reflection on what important next steps you can take in your context. As Irving and her team of researchers assert, "We cannot control the occurrence of Traumatic Stress, but we do exercise control over the systems and structures that support the missionaries we do send."[32] With this perspective, let us commit to supporting the leaders who supervise global workers well.

KIMBERLY DRAGE serves Novo UK (novouk.org) in organization-member relations. As a researcher, coach, and collaborator, she devotes herself to supporting the vital role of organizational health in global worker well-being. She has been ministering overseas (Asia and Europe) since 2006.

HYON KIM serves with SIM International (sim.org) as the global director of people development. She previously worked as a palliative care physician and assistant professor at the University of Toronto. Hyon and her husband served as medical missionaries in Niger, West Africa. She received her medical degree and training from the University of Toronto, Master of Theological Studies from Tyndale University & Seminary, and Master of Public Health from Johns Hopkins University

---

31 See the "Reporting Concerns" page from SIL as an excellent example. Rather than being hidden in the recesses of a policy manual, a quick google search will take you here, https://www.sil.org/reporting-concerns.

32 Irvine, Armentrout, and Miner, "Traumatic Stress," 327–36.

Questions for Reflection

- How has your perspective on the role of supervisory relationships and worker well-being changed after reading this chapter?
- What new awareness are you taking away from this chapter that you can apply to your own context?
- What is the role of connectedness in supervisory relationships? How can Scripture and your relationship with God better inform your understanding of supervisory relationships?
- How might organizations and member care departments, specifically, support the supervisory relationships within their organizations?

Additional Resources

Bremner, David. *Images of Leadership: Biblical Portraits of Godly Leaders*. Oasis International, 2021.

Center for Institutional Courage, https://www.institutionalcourage.org/the-call-to-courage.

Edmondson, Amy C. *The Fearless Organization: Creating Psychological Safety in the Workplace for Learning, Innovation, and Growth*. United Kingdom: Wiley, 2018.

Inceoglu, Ilke, Geoff Thomas, Chris Chu, David Plans, and Alexandra Gerbasi. "Leadership Behavior and Employee Well-Being: An Integrated Review and a Future Research Agenda." *The Leadership Quarterly* 29, no. 1 (February 1, 2018): 179–202. https://doi.org/10.1016/j.leaqua.2017.12.006.

Kelloway, E. Kevin and Julian Barling. "Leadership Development as an Intervention in Occupational Health Psychology." *Work & Stress* 24, no. 3 (July 1, 2010): 260–79. https://doi.org/10.1080/02678373.2010.518441.

Kurtessis, J.N., R. Eisenberger, M.T. Ford, L.C. Buffardi, K.A. Stewart, and C.S. Adis. "Perceived Organizational Support: A Meta-Analytic Evaluation of Organizational Support Theory." *Journal of Management* 43, no. 6 (2017): 1854–84. https://doi.org/10.1177/0149206315575554.

Luchman, Joseph N., and M. Gloria González-Morales. "Demands, Control, and Support: A Meta-Analytic Review of Work Characteristics Interrelationships." *Journal of Occupational Health Psychology* 18, no. 1 (2013): 37–52. https://doi.org/10.1037/a0030541.

Modini, Matthew, Sadhbh Joyce, Arnstein Mykletun, Helen Christensen, Richard A Bryant, Philip B Mitchell, and Samuel B Harvey. "The Mental Health Benefits of Employment: Results of a Systematic Meta-Review." *Australasian Psychiatry* 24, no. 4 (January 15, 2016): 331–36. https://doi.org/10.1177/1039856215618523.

Parker, Christopher P., Boris B. Baltes, Scott A. Young, Joseph W. Huff, Robert A. Altmann, Heather A. LaCost, and Joanne E. Roberts. "Relationships between Psychological Climate Perceptions and Work Outcomes: A Meta-Analytic Review." *Journal of Organizational Behavior* 24, no. 4 (2003): 389–416.

Rhoades, Linda and Robert Eisenberger. "Perceived Organizational Support: A Review of the Literature." *Journal of Applied Psychology* 87, no. 4 (2002): 698–714. https://doi.org/10.1037/0021-9010.87.4.698.

Wilder, E. James. *The Pandora Problem: Facing Narcissism in Leaders and Ourselves.* United States: Deeper Walk International, 2018.

Zhang, Yucheng, and Zhenyu Liao. "Consequences of Abusive Supervision: A Meta-Analytic Review." *Asia Pacific Journal of Management* 32, no. 4 (December 1, 2015): 959–87. https://doi.org/10.1007/s10490-015-9425-0.

CHAPTER 11

Personal and Spiritual Problems Can Cause Legal Ones

By Theresa Sidebotham

CARING FOR MISSION PERSONNEL presents incredible complexities. Common problems can include child harm, morality issues, toxic personalities, and mental health problems. Mistakes in approaching problems often involve communication failures and inappropriate confidentiality. Good policy approaches, training, sufficient documentation, and proactive responses to complaints are all part of healthy approaches to member care.

On-going problems and the level of emotional energy and resources required to respond to them can be discouraging. However, personnel issues present an opportunity to create healthy cultures and build the kingdom within the organization as well as reaching outward to the world with the gospel.

Child Harm on Several Levels

Mission agencies often think of child safety in terms of preventing or responding to child abuse, which is certainly important. But harm can also happen in other ways that may be less understood, such as through the educational environment or exposure to trauma.

Personnel issues present an opportunity to create healthy cultures and build the kingdom within the organization as well as reaching outward to the world with the gospel.

The risk of child abuse can increase with a poor understanding of cultural norms, perhaps in an unfamiliar culture. Let's look at a situation with a busy young family away from their home culture and in a difficult ministry area.

Their preschool daughter is invited on a play date with another little girl from the local community. The adult in charge of the playdate is the father of the other little girl. This is not in line with local cultural norms, but they do not realize it. When their daughter comes home, she describes being sexually molested.

If parents or leaders don't understand potential dangers present in the location of service or who in the local culture engages in child care, children can be put at risk of abuse. Naivete increases potential harm.

Abuse can also come from within families. For example, a couple discovers that their son and daughter have engaged in some sexual play. They discuss it with them, but do not report it to their mission or get treatment. Later, they learn that the behavior has become serious and compulsive, requiring ongoing specialized help.

Parents often don't know that child-on-child abuse, even within families, is a leading child safety issue. If they ignore the signs, or do not respond well when they become aware of a problem, ongoing harm can result.

In another scenario, a couple believes they are called to a remote location which requires homeschooling for their children. Their daughter learns to read easily and does her studies with little supervision, but her younger brother struggles. Neither parent has teacher training, and they do not know how to address their son's needs.

At the age of 10, the couple's son is diagnosed with processing problems. Because his parents did not seek early intervention, his future academic success is severely impaired. When the mission agency caring for this family tries to intervene, the couple has a strongly negative reaction.

Parents may not have realistic assessments of their children's educational needs or how they can be met. A child may have disabilities, diagnosed or not, that can lead to educational failure. Parents may also be overly optimistic about their ability to provide a quality homeschool program that meets their children's varying educational needs.

Other child harm concerns could arise when parents want to go to a dangerous location, saying they feel called there, up to and including martyrdom. Consider the couple that takes their two small children to a remote location that is sliding into civil war. When war breaks out, the family experiences an attack on the city. They flee to a bomb shelter to escape shelling. When they try to leave the country, the father is murdered in front of his family. The mother gets out with the children, but all of them now suffer from PTSD and long-term trauma.

In situations like these, could or should mission agencies have done something differently? What level of responsibility does a mission have for parents' choices? If a mission allows parents to remove a child from the support of his or her own culture (educationally, for child safety, or for cultural stability), does the mission have any obligation to speak into the situation? If adult children come back to a mission to ask why harm to them was allowed, what appropriate response can the mission make?

Spiritual Formation in the Mission's Values and Morality Issues

There has been a seismic shift in the cultural mores of the West, particularly around sexual issues. We often assume that evangelicals have similar moral values (such as not having sexual relationships outside of a monogamous marriage between a biological man and a biological woman), but that is a dangerous assumption. Many modern evangelicals don't have an issue with premarital sex and may also excuse other types of sexual encounters. The organization may have a statement of faith and code of conduct, but wrongly assumes that its members clearly understand (and agree with) its application.

For example, let's consider a young single woman who starts dating local men shortly after arriving on the field. About a month later, she reports to her mission that she has been sexually assaulted. She explains she was getting a nude massage from her date when the assault happened. This dating situation does not align with the intention of the mission's moral code. Furthermore, in this cultural context, this scenario would be considered an invitation for further sexual contact. How can mission personnel both provide care for her and deal with the moral failing?

In another situation a young single missionary arrives on the field and receives cultural orientation on relationships between men and women in the local context. Not long afterwards, she knowingly flirts with a married local man. As the relationship goes on, they meet alone, and he rapes her. In addition to personal trauma, the assault creates trauma for the team and damage to their testimony in the community.

When mission personnel talk with the young woman about her behavior and tell her she will not be allowed to return to the location, she files a lawsuit. Her suit alleges the mission retaliated against a victim of sexual assault.

These morality problems are two-fold. First, the moral code of

Spiritual formation around moral conduct, moral issues, and cultural considerations must be done ahead of time to be effective.

conduct is not understood, or if understood, was not accepted. Then, once a negative situation happens, it becomes almost impossible for the mission to provide spiritual or employment discipline without either worsening the trauma or creating a legal claim. It is also very difficult to provide both needed discipline and needed support.

What can missions do to prevent these situations? Mission leaders cannot make assumptions about shared values anymore. Spiritual formation around moral conduct, moral issues, and cultural considerations must be done ahead of time to be effective. And likely this guidance will have to be quite explicit.

Toxic Personalities in the Ministry World

Many people in ministry are humble and self-sacrificing. Yet ministries also attract toxic personalities: narcissists, sociopaths, and takers. Consider this example. A mission has a charismatic missionary who is an excellent pioneer and fundraiser. He always has plenty of money to fund whatever he wants. He is also a notorious rule-breaker, but this is tolerated because of his talent and productivity.

Over the years, people report that he lies and manipulates people. Several women also accuse him of harassment or boundary violations. But he comes across as so godly and trustworthy that the complaints are not believed. One day, irrefutable proof of sexual immorality emerges. Further investigation shows that for years, he has been sexually abusive towards women, and spiritu-

Responding well to early complaints may prevent more serious abuse.

ally abusive towards everyone.

At times, there can be less accountability in the nonprofit sector than the corporate world, and humble, self-sacrificing people can be easy to manipulate. Sometimes, talented and charismatic people may also be insubordinate, self-absorbed, manipulative, or liars.

Here's another scenario to think about. A group of field workers files a joint complaint that alleges a couple in leadership regularly insults and bullies both national and expatriate workers. An investigation confirms the complaint and uncovers a decades-long pattern of abuse. When the couple is removed from leadership, they email many people, including a prolific blogger, about the action. They claim their removal was unfair and motivated by jealousy. The blogger posts an article online that repeats the couple's claim. When it goes viral, the mission experiences a public backlash and a reduction in financial gifts.

Organizations often have unspoken rules that confronting people on bad behavior is not spiritual or poor form. Toxic people also tend to be skilled at managing conflict and work situations to make themselves look good. They may counter-attack to position themselves as the victim. This collision of the naïve and the toxic can lead to spiritual abuse and harm in ministries.

How can these situations be prevented? Being brilliant and successful should not give someone a pass to lie, manipulate, or misuse people or money. Complaints should be taken seriously and investigated, and standards should be applied equally to all. Responding well to early complaints may prevent more serious abuse.

Disabilities and Mental Health Issues

What about when missionaries or members of their family have disabilities or mental health concerns? When employees or applicants have disabilities, it triggers a special set of considerations. Let's look at an example of a young missionary known for difficult interactions. His quarrels with national church leaders and expatriate colleagues become infamous.

Over time, his anger turns more to withdrawal. He attempts suicide and is hospitalized for treatment. When he is released, he is put on a member care plan that requires psychological treatment. He is angry that leaders were made aware of his mental health problems. He resigns and files a claim of disability discrimination and invasion of privacy.

These considerations are even more complicated when disabilities relate to the mental health issues of children. Imagine a scenario where a teenage student at a missionary school explodes in rage and storms out of class when his teacher asks him for an assignment. When the teacher follows up with a meeting with the student and his parents, the student suddenly shouts, "I'm going to kill everyone here!"

His mother takes him from the room, and his father tells the teacher that their son just wants attention. The incident gets reported to the mission, and the family is sent home. The parents participate in a debrief, but then refuse to participate in recommended professional psychological care. They insist after furlough that their son is fine, and they want to return to the field.

How do missions prepare for these problems? Missions can evaluate their placements and job descriptions to see where they can (or cannot) accommodate people with mental health issues or other disabilities. Where are treatment and support available? Does that rule out certain locations? What teams have more resources to support people? How much attention will that take from other work?

Besides the employment paradigm of disability and accommodations, religious organizations can use a different paradigm – that of spiritual maturity. Ministries can require certain standards of spiritual maturity and fitness, measured in whether people treat each other in a biblical way (being humble, patient, kind, loving, forgiving). They can use this to screen out people lacking these character traits.

Situations where psychological help may be needed for either workers or their children should be handled carefully to prevent claims of disability discrimination. Adequate support should also be provided where possible (and where it is not possible, that should also be identified).

Sexual Orientation and Gender Identification (SOGI) Discrimination

Due to changing cultural values, missions must consider how to handle applicants or personnel struggling with SOGI issues. Given the current state of the law, the organization will likely need a spiritual statement of belief and a code of conduct based in Scripture.

If organizations have a traditional view of morality, they must also address whether they will take people who struggle in these areas but have committed not to live out that lifestyle. Or are these struggles disqualifying? Or if not fundamentally disqualifying, do they present too much risk? These issues are complex and likely need input from qualified legal counsel and consultants in psychology.

Failure to Communicate – Member Care, HR, and Leadership

Member care teams can provide support and resources for people in difficult situations that can help staff continue ministry.

Leadership cannot promote and position the right people without adequate information.

Sometimes, however, they also enable people by failing to share information that should go to HR and leadership, or supporting them for too long when they are really not functioning.

Let's look at this situation. A married man has been involved in on-going sexual sin including an affair with a man. A member care worker provides informal counseling to the man and his wife, but the worker does not have sufficient training to address the issues. The husband spends most sessions blaming his wife for his problems. No one informs leadership of the situation, and the couple continues in ministry for years. The wife eventually leaves her husband and the mission, saying she is traumatized.

In another case, a missionary couple comes home from the field after the wife physically attacks her husband. While a member care team is aware of ongoing domestic disputes, they do not disclose this to HR which is organizationally separate. Eventually, the couple is promoted to leadership. The wife becomes insubordinate to her supervisor. When she is disciplined, the couple resigns and files a lawsuit for gender discrimination and retaliation. This leads to anguish and loss of money for the mission.

Situations like this can be addressed by making sure that personnel problems get into personnel files and that leadership is made aware of them for performance reviews. Leadership cannot promote and position the right people without adequate information. And information that is held closely by member care workers is still imputed to the organization and can create legal liability down the road. This raises the question of what type of confidentiality is promised.

Role of Confidentiality

What is the role of confidentiality in this process? Sometimes, member care operates on a *counseling* model seeing people served as *clients*, and therefore communication is *privileged/confidential*. This may be stated explicitly or just assumed. (Sometimes this is expected even when the official policy says the opposite.)

Because member care departments and teams are agents of an organization, complete confidentiality is dangerous and should not be promised. Within the mission, the standard should be *need-to-know*. For therapist-patient confidentiality, missionaries should go to an outsider.

HR has its own obligations with respect to confidentiality and is required to keep personnel files confidential. Personnel files should contain ongoing records of issues that could be important later. Leaders should also regularly get important information on a need-to-know basis. This way, problems can be addressed rather than hidden, forgotten, or assumed (each time) to be fixed. This can also prevent people from getting leadership roles for which they do not have spiritual or emotional maturity.

Proactive Legal and Policy Protections

In the United States, and to a greater or lesser extent in other jurisdictions, religious organizations have some protections to hire people with ministerial qualifications. In the US, particularly, organizations should document carefully who the ministers are, put in place spiritual standards for all jobs, and have clear codes of conduct.

Spiritual traits should be required from personnel, especially for leadership roles. Expectations of general moral conduct, and particularly of child safety conduct, should also be clear. This allows organizations to apply their faith-based standards in holding people accountable.

Another way to protect the organization, in jurisdictions where employment contracts are common, is to include good cause reasons to terminate a contract. For example, those could include failure in complying with child safety standards.

Consider having agreements (in some jurisdictions) that conflicts will be resolved by Christian mediation under Scriptural principles, or at least that people agree to try that process first.

Good HR Practices and Documentation

Leaders as well as HR personnel should be trained in good HR practices. It's common for excited leaders dealing with personnel problems to accidentally say something that can be the foundation for a discrimination lawsuit.

Documenting performance problems is important, especially if they go on over a long period of time. When a person must be disciplined or terminated, this provides the needed justification for the action.

On the other hand, if it's clear that a person has problematic performance or behavior, it's usually best to terminate them rather than let the situation get more complicated and messier. This decision should also be adequately documented. Any spiritual standards relied on should be included.

Responding and Investigating

Part of handling personnel issues is to receive grievances well, take them seriously, and investigate when that is needed. Some claims, such as of child safety or sexual harassment or other forms of discrimination, must be investigated and can lead to liability if not addressed. (For child safety problems, appropriate outside reporting is also required.)

Other complaints should also be earnestly considered, both to create a good working culture, and to make sure there isn't a pattern developing in the situation. Responding can be simple and informal (for less serious allegations) or may require a formal investigation.

Depending on the seriousness of the situation and the talent available within the organization, investigations may be internal or external. A poorly done investigation may cause more problems than it solves. Investigating is a sophisticated skill that requires training. The organization may also need legal help.

Training

Prioritizing training is an important way for organizations to reduce liability. Member care providers need to be taught how to respond to mental health issues, handle moral/spiritual problems, and share appropriately with HR and leadership. HR leaders need help implementing good HR practices and support to stay up to date on the law. Organizational leaders should also be trained in resolving problems, including when to work closely with HR. Finally, everyone in every organization should be educated in areas such as child protection, sexual harassment, general discrimination, how to make complaints, and spiritual formation. The proactive measure ensure organizational health well into the future.

THERESA LYNN SIDEBOTHAM founded Telios Law (telioslaw.com) in 2012, where she helps ministries, churches, businesses, and individuals to fulfill their calling, representing them in investigations, litigation, and alternatives to litigation, as well as giving legal advice on a variety of issues. Theresa also directs Telios Teaches, an affiliate company that provides online training for ministries and secular organizations in sexual harassment prevention, child protection, and other HR issues.

Questions for Reflection

- Are spiritual standards for behavior in leadership, on teams, and in other interpersonal situations clear and enforceable in your ministry?
- Is your child protection and HR training current and consistent with your biblical values?
- Do your leaders have both the training and courage to walk through difficult personnel problems?

Additional Resources

Evangelical Council for Abuse Prevention. "Child Safety Standards." https://ecap.net/standards/.

Telios Teaches. Training from Tellios Law PLLC: Employees are happier and healthier when they are protected. See HR, Child Safety, and Professional Development training at https://teliosteaches.com/.

Telios Teaches. Protect Those in Your Care:

Child protection, investigation, and response. https://telios.site/investigationgiveaway.

Telios Teaches. Purchase an annual subscription at https://telios.site/studio.

Telios Teaches. Free resources and blogs from Telios Law and Telios Teaches. https://teliosteaches.com/blog.

Sidebotham, Theresa L. *Handling Allegations in a Ministry: Responses and Investigations*. Illumify Media, 2022.

CHAPTER 12

Reframing Sabbatical Posture in the Post-Pandemic Landscape

By Jeff and Sara Simons

THE PROTESTANT WORK ETHIC has profoundly shaped the cultural landscape especially for North Americans serving in ministry. On the positive side, it encourages hard work to achieve measurable goals. However, its *shadow side* sets aside or reduces God's good gift of rest. Areas like self-care, work/life balance, sufficient and restorative vacations, and God's command and model for us to engage healthy and regular *sabbatical* rhythms hardly exist.

We often hear from North American cross-cultural workers that they find healthier models for work/life balance and community vitality in their host cultures. This was true of our experience living and working in Spain. Family, community, and time to recharge are values held in high esteem. That could be observed in how people used their time, planned their daily schedules, as well in the abundance of public space devoted to communal gathering.

The *refreshment* we receive in our routines and spiritual disciplines is critical. Yet deeper *renewal* is needed and can only come in the breadth and depth of a longer season like a sabbatical. The condition we often refer to as *burnout* is subtle and gradual and can happen when we don't strategically plan for renewal. It can deplete us to such a degree that *devotional times* become simply wafting fumes into our already empty tanks. We can start to lose sight of ourselves and God. As Mark Buchanan points out in his book, *The Rest of God*, "We can be very busy for God and still not know him."[1]

Walter Brueggemann, in *Sabbath as Resistance*, talks about sabbath as a pause that transforms. It is to cease even for a short time from anxious striving to find ourselves again with a light burden. While a weekly sabbath provides pause to reflect on the burdens we carry, often it is only enough to acknowledge our tiredness and striving rather than take an honest inventory, time for deep rest, and renewal. Only after a time of rest can we truly reflect and consider what rhythms will carry us into a healthier future.[2]

A group of culinary experts in northern Spain have turned the sabbatical concept on its head. Every year, the staff of the Michelin-star restaurant, *El Bulli,* receive a 6-month sabbatical! The restaurant closes for half the year for *all* of the staff! The time is used for rest, vacation, play, renewed energy and creativity, research, and space to dream about new cutting-edge culinary innovations.

Closing for half the year risks major revenue losses, yet it fuels creative ideas that change the worldwide culinary landscape, placing them securely as a frontrunner of ingenuity for others to follow. Their counter-cultural example has brought about phenomenal success![3]

This example, while extreme, should cause us to consider: *what if we actually took God's command for sabbatical seriously,*

---

1 Mark Buchanan, *The Rest of God: Restoring Your Soul by Restoring Sabbath* (Nashville, TN: Thomas Nelson Publishers, 2007), 181.

2 Walter Brueggemann, *Sabbath as Resistance: Saying No to the Culture of Now* (Westminster John Knox Press, 2014).

3 J.P. Solano, "How El Bulli restaurant turned dining into an experience – a UX case study," *UX Design* (online), November 19, 2014, https://uxdesign.cc/how-elbulli-turned-dining-into-an-experience-38f1c015e9f6.

What if we actually took God's command for sabbatical seriously, and allowed ourselves to think and interact with the Spirit in such creativity and abandon?

and allowed ourselves to think and interact with the Spirit in such creativity and abandon? Sabbatical rest is not just a good idea, a privilege to those in power, or only to be taken when we are limping and near burnout. Rather, a solid theology of rest and a pre-meditated rhythm for growth is a grand opportunity to foster lifelong resilience and provides fertile soil for ground-breaking kingdom innovation.

As Buchanan emphatically contends:

> Get this straight: The rest of God – the rest God gladly gives so that we might discover that part of God we're missing – is not a reward for finishing. It's not a bonus for work well done. It's a sheer gift. It is a stop-work order in the midst of work that's never complete, never polished. Sabbath is not the break we're allotted at the tail end of completing all our tasks and chores, the fulfillment of all our obligations. It's the rest we take smack-dab in the middle of them, without apology, without guilt, and for no better reason than God told us we could.[4]

The world after the COVID-19 pandemic is full of exhausted ministry leaders which makes this a timely opportunity to reframe sabbatical practice. To recover, build resiliency, and respond to

---

4 Buchanan, *The Rest of God*, 92.

A tsunami of burnout may be just beginning to swell if preventative measures are not put in place.

the seismic shifts happening globally, missional workers and leaders must embrace, leverage, and develop well-planned and effective sabbatical rhythms, for themselves, their teams, their organizations, and their churches.

The Swelling Tsunami: Post-pandemic Burnout

For around 10 years, *sabbatical coaching* was a *secondary* part of our work as transition specialists. However, as the global COVID-19 pandemic violently hurled many into difficult and undesired transitions, our sabbatical coaching work exponentially expanded.

We saw cross-cultural workers displaced by governments that used COVID as an excuse to remove foreigners. We witnessed workers use extreme agility to totally re-invent how to *minister* without being able to gather. We observed families split up for months due to country border closures and lockdowns. We walked alongside many as they traversed through a long tunnel of confusion and grief after constant disruptions and changes that came without opportunities for closure. As ministry leaders stumbling out of this, we wonder: how is a *healthy* and *sustainable* life of ministry even possible in today's world? A tsunami of burnout may be just beginning to swell if preventative measures are not put in place.

A Barna report from March 2022 showed that pastors in the US are struggling with burnout at unprecedented levels. It showed that 42% of pastors across the board and 46% of pastors under the age of 45 are considering quitting full-time ministry. It further revealed that burnout levels among female clergy outpaced their male counterparts.[5]

Global ministry leaders share many of the same vulnerabilities for burnout as the pastors in this report including:

- Caring for bereaved people in an unusually dark season without support for their own sorrows.
- Navigating difficult conversations about polarized and politically-charged topics related to the pandemic, gender diversity, and social justice issues.
- Holding onto unrealistically high expectations from those they serve and for themselves.
- Providing evidence to donors and congregants of outcomes to prove that their *investment* is producing a good *return*.
- Experiencing intensified isolation, and long-term heavy emotions which turn into chronic stress.

The common thread has been exhausting feelings of isolation and a lack of permission, by self and others, to separate from their role as ministry leaders for a season of renewal. As Robert C. Saler points out: "Pastors and ministry leaders care at a very deep level, about a great many people, at the most intense points of those peoples' lives."[6]

Unhealthy ministry enmeshment creeps in subtly, posing first as courageous commitment. Then it slowly sours into a trap where love for God and others is at risk of being lost. Many wear their exhaustion as a false badge of honor. However, over time significant burnout leads most ministry leaders to give up their *call* to full-time mission engagement. Few make it back.

---

5 Tish Harrison Warren, "Why Pastors are Burning Out," *New York Times*, August 26, 2022, https://www.nytimes.com/2022/08/28/opinion/pastor-burnout-pandemic.html.

6 Robert C. Saler, *Planning Sabbaticals: A Guide for Congregations and Their Pastors* (St. Louis, MO: Chalice Press, 2019), 9.

Organizations and donors make significant investments in each ministry worker's preparation and work in their areas of kingdom call. This should make it all the more important to try to counteract this mostly unnecessary attrition. But how can we help prevent and facilitate recovery from burnout?

My (Jeff's) own journey toward burnout began when I was engaged in full-time, cross-cultural ministry. My work had been a decent fit for 7 years, but I was still spiraling downward. I experienced a *holy discontent* with my current ministry roles/ activities. They no longer fully fit. I felt nudged towards greater leadership responsibilities, and new visions and dreams, confirmed by others, began to blossom. Over time, this tension became unbearable.

However, I lacked the energy, fortitude, and perspective to make any sustainable major changes. The way forward was unclear. My sleep was frequently interrupted by anxious thoughts about how to figure this out, and the knot in my stomach grew more constant. Typically, a gregarious extrovert, I grew more and more annoyed by others, and wanted to withdraw from everyone. My impatience boiled up easily and regularly, particularly with my wife and kids.

All of this eventually led me into my first sabbatical. Sabbaticals provide a great path to balance, health, long-term resiliency of call, and finding oneself securely rooted again in the identity of Christ. As Buchanan aptly notes: "In a culture where busyness is a fetish and stillness is laziness, rest is sloth. But without rest, we miss the rest of God."[7]

There is much to gain from this gift of pause and perspective shift. As Buchanan further writes, "Sabbath helps reorient us to our work. It is an opportunity to step back far enough from what we do to look at it objectively and ask, Is this what I was sent to do? Am I on course? Is this my food?"[8]

---

7 Buchanan, *The Rest of God*, 3.

8 Buchanan, *The Rest of God*, 170.

A well-planned and embraced sabbatical season offers so many levels of strength and advantage. As Saler explains: "… To honor ministry is to strengthen it. To embrace rest is to demonstrate confidence in the energy that God can provide."[9]

Guiding Principles for Effective Sabbatical

To experience their true worth and impact, sabbaticals take a balance of planning well and letting go for the Spirit to lead. Intentional forethought, conversations with significant others, and discussions with leaders and mentors are all critical parts of planning. However, when we hold our sabbatical plans with open hands, the transformation God desires to take place becomes clearer. Here are key elements to think through.

INITIATE KEY CONVERSATIONS. Once you know that you are heading toward a sabbatical season, see what your organization or church allows, supports, or provides concerning sabbaticals. Many leaders are pleasantly surprised to find a provided structure, or even funding for development or care that can help offset sabbatical costs.

REFINE COMMUNICATION. A healthy sabbatical not only incorporates rest and renewal, but reflection, learning, deepening, and clarity towards fresh vision. If semantics create barriers to understanding, we encourage workers to talk about a sabbatical as a season for both *intentional leadership development* and *improved health and resilience*. Ideally, this is a nonproduction-oriented time. We find that more people of all sectors can understand and support a sabbatical when it is defined with well-articulated language and measurable goals. Goals should include rest at the onset and life-giving activities all throughout.

---

9 Saler, *Planning Sabbaticals*, 9.

This set-aside time allows for freedom for in-depth self-exploration and intentional development.

ENGAGE OTHERS IN PRAYER. Engaging a small prayer team during a sabbatical season is non-negotiable. This temporary group of trust-worthy companions can pray against distractions, voices from the past, against discouragement and towards beneficial life-giving rhythms. Sending them regular communication with more specific requests as well as answers to prayer can be a life-line during a sabbatical.

LOOK FOR PROFESSIONALS. This set-aside time allows for freedom for in-depth self-exploration and intentional development. Consider targeted interaction with professionals to help you prepare for the future. A pastor, spiritual director, medical professional, athletic trainer, counselor, or marriage therapist or any combination of those professionals or others can aide specific areas of desired growth, maturity, and wholeness.

WORK WITH A SABBATICAL COACH. We strongly recommend enlisting a competent sabbatical coach in your process. A coach can listen to your unique needs, co-create a blueprint plan based on your desires for renewal and growth, coach you toward action steps, and provide accountability with regular check-ins. They can also keep your bigger sabbatical plan in mind so you can stay focused on your current week or month with the appropriate rhythms and disciplines crafted for that section of the sabbatical.

BREAK IT INTO MANAGEABLE PHASES FOR SUCCESS. Planning can feel overwhelming in burnout, so working with a structure can be helpful. We suggest 6 phases, so you can focus on one small part at a time. In our approach, we include pre- and post- phases that allow for healthy *off-ramping* into sabbatical, space for properly debriefing your sabbatical, and then time for *on-ramping* after sabbatical that allows for incremental re-engagement.

CAREFULLY CHOOSE SABBATICAL LENGTH, TIMING, AND PLACE. In general, we suggest that workers do not take less than a three-month sabbatical in order to have time for necessary phases of a sabbatical. Saler suggests, "3–4 months of unbroken time away is ideal; this allows for the gift of time to live into patterns of rest and refocus. This minimum amount of time is often the thing that produces the most potent transformation."[10]

However, if you or your spouse have experienced burnout or major interpersonal strife and need to engage deeper professional services (medical and/or counseling), or you need time for more significant vocational discernment, a longer season of sabbatical is advised. Six to twelve months often serves people more adequately.

No one we have worked with has ever felt like their sabbatical was too long for what they needed! Almost everyone feels like the time they planned out ended up being too short. Let that be a consideration in your own planning.

You will also want to think when and where you do your sabbatical. For example, will you take a sabbatical at the same time as your spouse? Will your sabbatical be timed in a particular way with your children's school schedules? Will you stay in your primary location for all or most of the time? Limiting travel to a couple of strategic trips can serve you better than frequent travel during a sabbatical. The same careful consideration applies to hosting visitors.

---

10 Saler, *Planning Sabbaticals*, 18.

PLAN HOLISTIC RHYTHMS INTO YOUR PHASES. Some holistic rhythms will be appropriate for the entirety of your sabbatical; others will be pertinent to one or two phases only. Craft disciplines into the phases of your sabbatical according to your needs, and be flexible with them. As Buchanan explains, think of disciplines during sabbatical "as choreography notes. They are not to be followed slavishly. They are hints and prompts and invitations. They're meant to try to coax you onto the dance floor, to help you limber up, to get you to move in ways you might at first think awkward or foolhardy."[11]

REPORT EFFECTIVELY. The process of consolidating and communicating your learning provides an important overview of the entirety of your time. Steve Hoke suggests creating a summary of how your sabbatical met or did not meet your goals. This will help colleagues and your organization understand the value of this time. In addition, reporting back to family, friends or colleagues is a way of thanking them for the sacrifices they likely made in your absence.[12]

Sabbatical Posture as Leverage for Kingdom Growth

Missiologist and theologian Charles E. Van Engen frequently reminds his students, "If the theology of the ivory tower does not become the theology of the sidewalk, it ceases to be theology."[13] His admonishment has particular poignancy in this post-COVID period.

In this *time-between-the-times*, we must consider what the

---

11 Buchanan, *The Rest of God*, 11.

12 Steve Hoke, "Taking Sabbaticals Seriously," in *Global Mission Handbook: A Guide For Cross-cultural Service*, by Steve Hoke and Bill Taylor (Downers Grove, IL: Intervarsity Press, 2009), 258.

13 Charles E. Van Engen, "MT537: Theologizing in Mission" (course lecture notes, Fuller Theological Seminary, School of Intercultural Studies, Winter 2002).

Craft disciplines into the phases of your sabbatical according to your needs, and be flexible with them.

workers of the harvest need. How do we steward these precious human resources well? How do we mature and cultivate spiritual disciplines of resilience for lifelong kingdom impact? Not only can we model how to do this for the church and the world, this can become a key leveraging force for missional growth in the world's changing landscape.

We see the highest attrition of workers after 3–5 years in their new ministry – when ministry momentum and growth are usually starting to bloom! What if the leadership burnout, abandonment, and train-wrecks that we too often observe could be intercepted with a well-developed sabbatical rhythm?

What if sabbaticals could become the tool for fueling *budding shoots* of ministry into mature growth? Healthy sabbatical rhythms are the overlooked discipline that can catalyze healthy and effective missional leaders for decades to come. In this very turbulent and confusing era, leaders of every context need to consider how effective sabbatical practice can work for them.

SARA AND JEFF SIMONS provide resources and support for the development of ministry leaders in major transition through The Way Between (thewaybetween.org). They have served in this way for over 20 years. After living abroad for 11 years, including eight years in Spain, they now live in Colorado with their two children. They both hold master's degrees in intercultural studies and leadership, bachelor's degrees in psychology, and ICF coaching credentials.

Questions for Reflection

- In what physical, emotional, relational, communal, familial, and spiritual ways did the COVID-19 pandemic affect you?
- What is the current reading on your resiliency meter? Where is it in relation to your need for *refreshment* (regular spiritual disciplines in your week), and *renewal* (season for greater recuperation, more clarity for your call, and increased connection to God and yourself)?
- If you feel that you need more *renewal*, what is one next step you can take toward entering a sabbatical season?

Additional Resources

Sevier, Melissa Bane. *Journeying Toward Renewal: A Spiritual Companion for Pastoral Sabbaticals*. Bethesda, MD: Alban Institute, 2002.

Buchanan, Mark. *The Rest of God: Restoring Your Soul by Restoring Sabbath*. Nashville, TN: Thomas Nelson Publishers, 2007.

Barton, Ruth Haley. *Embracing Rhythms of Work and Rest: From Sabbath to Sabbatical and Back Again*. InterVarsity Press, 2023.

Saler, Robert C. *Planning Sabbaticals: A Guide for Congregations and Their Pastors*. St. Louis, MO: Chalice Press, 2019.

Swoboda, A.J. and Matthew Sleeth. *Subversive Sabbath: The Surprising Power of Rest in a Nonstop World*. Brazos Press, 2018.

Hoke, Steve and Bill Taylor. *Global Mission Handbook: A Guide For Cross-cultural Service*. Downers Grove, IL: Intervarsity Press, 2009.

Simons, Sara. *Sabbatical Planning Guide (digital)*.
Lakewood, CO: The Way Between, Inc, 2018. https://www.
thewaybetween.org/.

Simons, Sara and Jeff Simons. *Sabbaticals with Effective
Recovery and Upward Momentum*. Lakewood, CO: The Way
Between, Inc. https://www.thewaybetween.org/.

CHAPTER 13

Reframing Sabbatical Posture: Embodied and Developmental

By Sara and Jeff Simons

OVER THE YEARS, WE HAVE SEEN plenty of leaders *crash* or *collapse* into a sabbatical, usually spending the first month or two focused on accident recovery. While we don't recommend it, it is a step in the right direction! Embracing God's model for sabbatical remains a restorative space for these times. In fact, sometimes sudden and unavoidable events can become major factors that lead us into needed sabbatical seasons and personal leave.

However, ideally, we could all be intentional about a preventative and rhythmic sabbatical schedule that connects us deeply with God before we reach desperate places of burnout, interpersonal conflict ruptures, or veering way outside our call and giftedness. The most successful leaders do not just *stumble* into a sabbatical. Healthy leaders know what they need, and are not afraid to ask for it, or pursue it. They intentionally plan it as part of a posture of lifelong learning and leadership development.

Chronic stress has physical and emotional ramifications. It can take years to see its impact because it builds subtly. But eventually, we will experience depletion in multiple parts of our lives: physically, emotionally, spiritually, relationally, socially, and in our family. The purposeful and holistic renewal that a

The COVID-19 pandemic challenged nearly every global worker individually and communally at an embodied level.

sabbatical offers can counteract this, but it usually requires more space, grace, cushion, and margin than you may think.

Embodied Development

On our own sabbatical journeys, we quickly realized that our whole bodies needed renewal. A sabbatical season that addressed all of these areas was not only a healthy response, but a posture that led us to a new level of awareness about ourselves, and God. It put us in a place not just for *renewal*, but it forwarded our development into the next season of leadership that God had for us.[1]

One way we evaluate leaders considering a sabbatical season is through a *sabbatical readiness survey* and an in-take conversation. Through this tool, we can see how much renewal is needed in each facet of life and work with leaders to determine the best ways to craft their sabbatical season to best meet their needs.

The COVID-19 pandemic challenged nearly every global worker individually and communally at an embodied level. For many, it pushed their exhaustion and burn out levels to a critical state needing attention. A sabbatical that seeks various methods of embodiment, whole-brain engagement, creativity, play, learning, time to encounter God, and communal interaction and input can

---

[1] We want to express appreciation to the Navigators organization (navigators. org), for the years of groundwork they've done in creating practical guides for workers engaging in sabbatical practice. Their tools provided our initial introduction to this topic.

be a necessary way to replenish, restore, and rebuild.

Interpersonal conflict and difficult vocational decisions catalyzed my (Sara's) first sabbatical. Reading and engaging in mental exercises, which usually provided me with refreshment, became taxing and difficult. To receive the Lord's restoration, he led me to non-verbal and non-written practices. I was to draw it out, hike it out, experiment with different prayer postures and exercises that opened alternative connections with God and my whole self. It was a stretch! While my body had held me in this stressful time, it was now my turn to listen to it, learn from it, and speak the language of care in return.

Psychiatrist Bessel van der Kolk's powerful work, *The Body Keeps the Score,* highlights the strong connection between physical and mental health. Seasons of high stress, transition, or trauma can severely impair our mental processing and decision making as well as increase physical manifestations like pain or sleeplessness. In these times, we can feel trapped in a tunnel-vision spin cycle of repetitions thought, often hyper-focused on past struggles or future concerns. As van der Kolk points out, physical engagement can help us move through stress more effectively because it activates more of our brains than a cognitive approach.[2]

Engaging our bodies in movement and brains in creativity ignites the whole brain in helping us overcome blocks and mental stagnation. It also integrates our whole selves in the complex processes of transition. In *The Artist's Rule*, Christine Valters Paintner shares, "When I find myself feeling stuck for ideas and inspiration or feeling like my perspective has narrowed from fatigue, a walk can change everything–creating shifts, renewal and invigoration."[3]

This approach has shifted our own work patterns and rein-

---

2 Bessel van Der Kolk, *The Body Keeps the Score: Brain, Mind, and Body in the Healing of Trauma* (NY: Viking Press, 2014).

3 Christine Valters Paintner, *The Artist's Rule: Nurturing Your Creative Soul with Monastic Wisdom* (IN: Sorin Books, 2011), 17.

vented the way we lead ministry workers in sabbatical practices. We engage them first in exercises focused on breathing, connecting creatively with the Creator, simple art techniques, and body movement. One of the unique ways we help leaders in sabbatical seasons engage their whole being and deeper connection with God is on group spiritual pilgrimage treks along the Camino de Santiago.

And we strongly encourage *play*, which most of us lack in our everyday lives. This, too, activates whole brain functioning, leading to more effective and sustainable work for the long-haul. "Play lies at the core of creativity and innovation .... Play seems to be one of the most advanced methods nature has invented to allow a complex brain to create itself," contends Stuart Brown.[4]

Hobbies, sports, games, art, and simple play often get edged out in the heavy seriousness we bring to adult life. These necessary life-giving self-care elements create deeper levels of resilience and health and deepens our connection to our Creator. When they are neglected, it can wreak havoc on our already stressed systems, leading to greater problems.

Even the writer of Ecclesiastes reminds us that God takes pleasure in seeing us enjoy the earth that he created for us. One way we can experience his kingdom right now is by relishing the people and provisions around us – eating, drinking, and being merry in God's presence with us now! God has supplied what we need to be sustained and healthy, and he wants us to enjoy the gifts and talents he gives even if not purposed for ministry to others. Keeping this in balance with the rest of our lives is a spiritual discipline that breeds both gratitude and contentment.

Olympic track athlete and later missionary to China Eric Liddell expressed just this when he was asked why he wasted his time running when there was so much of the Lord's work to do. He responded that when he runs, he feels God's pleasure! His

---

4 Stuart Brown, *Play: How it Shapes the Brain, Opens the Imagination & Invigorates the Soul* (NY: Avery Publishing Group, 2011), 40.

God has supplied what we need to be sustained and healthy, and he wants us to enjoy the gifts and talents he gives even if not purposed for ministry to others

running was also an integrated part of living out how he was wired to be in this world.

Leadership Development

Sabbatical seasons are often transition periods between current kingdom involvement, and God's next level call. Sabbaticals should not be seen as an *easy road to moving on*, or a method for *quiet quitting*. We've discovered the opposite! They are spiritually rich and significantly transformative times that require a high learning curve. Regular sabbatical rhythms can offer a strategic advantage that usually leads to higher staff retention, increased organizational impact, and the improved stability and resiliency of a ministry.

Character formation and a stable sense of self are foundational for quality participation in ministry. Sabbaticals give workers permission for exploration, creation, listening, and space to consider who they are apart from work. The best thing an organization can do when they see a worker beginning to burn out or appearing to give up is to bless them with the space and time that a sabbatical affords. The worker will return to the organization with renewed creativity, or if he or she finds a new path, they will most likely depart speaking highly an organization that valued his or her contribution and development.

Buchanan asked himself a penetrating question on his sabbat-

Freed, focused, and clarified workers create momentum, pulse, healthy work teams, and improved work environments.

ical: "Do I want to get well? ... If I believe I'm to go back restored, in what ways am I sick now? And how have I grown content with that?"[5]

Sabbaticals that are submitted to the transformation of God in our lives move us through areas, known or unknown, that cripple us, stunt our impact, and can ultimately be part of breeding a negative culture in an organization. Freed, focused, and clarified workers create momentum, pulse, healthy work teams, and improved work environments.

Sometimes a sabbatical season is a key element of recuperation and renewal with God that is needed to do deeper discernment. Starting a sabbatical with a phase of rest can prepare you to enter into greater growth, awareness, and clarification about your kingdom impact.

However, adjusting to a sabbatical is often a rollercoaster, not a steady incline or decline. Those on sabbatical *all* experience a hangover, or angsty period. It can feel like detoxing – the addiction is adrenaline! You'll need stable support – even if you don't feel like having it.

Sabbatical coaches can provide that from the beginning by helping create a clear structure and set a general timeline that also allows space for flexibility. They can build your awareness of the factors or risks that can derail a quality sabbatical. And for those who *collapse* into a sabbatical season with little focus,

---

5 Mark Buchanan, *The Rest of God: Restoring Your Soul by Restoring Sabbath* (Nashville, TN: Thomas Nelson Publishers, 2007), 152.

motivation, and discipline, a coach can keep you on track.

After his post-pandemic sabbatical, a mission agency CEO and client of ours said, "Having a sabbatical coach was crucial to me getting the most out of the time. My coach helped me overcome the initial guilt of spending so much time resting and focusing on self-care, gave me a framework for goal setting and evaluation, led me in spiritual exercises of communing with God, and listened as I verbally processed. I would highly recommend an experienced coach to all my staff or anyone else as they enter a sabbatical!"

A developmental perspective on sabbatical can also help stakeholders such as donors, supporters, or a sending church that may not understand or support the idea of sabbaticals. Explaining that a healthy sabbatical is not only for rest and renewal, but also about reflection, learning, growing, clarity, and forming a fresh vision for future ministry can help them get on board. And our faithful God meets us during times of transformation and growth.

Developing an Effective Sabbatical Culture

We conducted a small survey among one hundred ministry leaders who had taken a sabbatical. Our results showed that while many shifted responsibilities or roles after a sabbatical to varying degrees, the majority stayed within their organization. Less than 10% left their organization altogether. And those that did leave, did so with heightened maturity, and greater clarity about where they can have the best kingdom impact. They left with *few* organizational complaints and *more* focus on their unique wiring and fit! From a *Missio Dei* perspective, that is a kingdom win to be celebrated by all!

As Buchanan describes it, sabbaticals are about finding health, balance, and growth while relinquishing the temptation to play God:

> ... indeed, the worst hallucination busyness conjures is the conviction that I am God. All depends on me. How will the right

things happen at the right time if I'm not pushing and pulling and watching and worrying! ... [I]f God can take any mess, any mishap, any wastage, any wreckage, any anything, and choreograph beauty and meaning from it, then you can take a day off. Either God's always at work, watching the city, building the house, or you need to try harder. Either God is good and in control, or it all depends on you .... [W]e mimic God in order to remember we're not God. In fact, that is a good definition of Sabbath: imitating God so that we stop trying to be God.[6]

Sabbaticals can provide holistic recovery, counteract high stress periods, and renew and enhance creativity. But what do healthy sabbatical rhythms for the staff of an organization look like? How does an organization develop a thriving sabbatical culture to increase its kingdom impact?

First recognize that burnout is not a holy badge of honor and then invest time in developing a more robust theology of sabbath rest. Organizational attitudes about sabbaticals likely need reframing around this more robust theology. Sabbaticals should be seen as part of a lifelong posture of rest that leads to kingdom resiliency for individuals and organizations.

Instead of looking at sabbaticals with fear that they will cause good staff to leave, they can be seen as a gift that forms workers for new and more dynamic kingdom opportunities that can increase organizational impact. Rather than being thought of as a way to quietly off-ramp workers on the way out, sabbatical rhythms should be viewed as periods of strategic growth to achieve greater alignment with an organization's mission.

Another step to consider would be to run a pilot program where organizational sabbatical rhythms can be trialed. This can help organizations see how sabbaticals impact operations in real time, which can help appropriate policies to be developed for them. It's important to keep in mind that sabbatical policies

---

6 Buchanan, *The Rest of God*, 61, 63.

Sabbatical rhythms should be viewed as periods of strategic growth to achieve greater alignment with an organization's mission.

should be approached with intentionality and cover more than just upper leadership levels.

A gifted team or body within an organization – typically *not* planted in the human resources department – should be charged with effectively rolling out sabbatical policies across an organization. They can aid leaders in navigating succession plans for their regions, departments, or teams that accommodate sabbatical rhythms. They can also help establish a bank of competent inside (or outside) sabbatical support that can be made available to staff. That can include recovery and development resources such as counseling, coaching, and spiritual direction.

Eventually sabbaticals should be made available to *all* staff and leveraged to regularly recalibrate staff to live into their unique wiring. Sabbaticals strategically honor both the organization's communal mission, and each person's growth trajectory and kingdom fit. Moving this direction ensures longer-lasting health and greater kingdom engagement. It also accepts God's invitation of rest and demonstrates its effects to the overly busy world around us.

SARA AND JEFF SIMONS provide resources and support for the development of ministry leaders in major transition through The Way Between (thewaybetween.org). They have served this way for over 20 years. After living abroad for 11 years, including eight years in Spain, they now live in Colorado with their two children. They both hold master's degrees in intercultural studies and leadership, bachelor's degrees in psychology, and ICF coaching credentials.

Questions for Reflection

- In what ways have you become aware of warning signals that point to your reserves getting too low, or your adrenaline running too high for too long?
- What methods of physical or creative engagement have you discovered or practiced to counteract stress and burnout? What new methods would you like to try?
- How could a more developmental approach to sabbaticals positively enhance your growth during your next sabbatical? How might this approach positively change your organization's culture?

Additional Resources

Nouwen, Henri J. M. *Sabbatical Journey: The Diary of His Final Year*. New York: The Crossroad Publishing Company, 2000.

Foster, Richard. *Celebration of Discipline, Special Anniversary Edition: The Path to Spiritual Growth*. San Francisco: HarperOne, 2018.

Van der Kolk, Bessel. *The Body Keeps the Score: Brain, Mind, and Body in the Healing of Trauma*. NY: Viking Press, 2014.

Valters Paintner, Christine. *The Artist's Rule: Nurturing Your Creative Soul with Monastic Wisdom*. Notre Dame, IN: Sorin Books, 2011.

CHAPTER 14

The Heart of Member Care

By Geoff Whiteman

"**WHY DO GLOBAL WORKERS IN CHRIST** need specialized care?" I asked a room full of therapists and psychiatrists who serve this population exclusively. We all serve with Valeo (valeo.global) – one of about a dozen organizations worldwide that provide clinical services for global Christian workers.[1]

Clinical care is one of many modalities for *member care*.[2] Other member care modalities include mentoring, life coaching, spiritual direction, and more. Member care professionals work in member care organizations, mission agencies, sending churches, or independently. They may go to where global workers live through visits or online, or welcome global workers into their centers or homes.

Professional development resources and training for member care abound. There are multiple conferences, courses, and degree programs for member care practitioners to grow in professional competence. This discipline has become an industry!

In 2023, we conducted a needs assessment as the first ini-

---

1 To honor those who live in *closed* or *creative access* countries it is common to avoid terms like *missionary*.

2 This is the phrase we often use to describe specialized care for global workers.

tiative of the Valeo Research Institute (valeo.global/research). The perspective of 175 member care professionals, directors, and concerned global workers were shared regarding the state of our discipline. The full results were presented at Missio Nexus' Mission Leader Conference that year and are available at valeo.global/research.

It was clear that love and professionalism drove participants' concerns about global workers in Christ well-being and development. They know the need is real because they see it. They are concerned about global workers personally because they love them and long to see them flourish. They want to serve them with excellence because they themselves received excellent care when they needed it most, or remember the trauma of its absence. Their hearts for global workers renew our vision.

In the flurry of activity, our vision is prone to drift. The youth pastor who discipled me said "The main thing is to keep the main thing, the main thing." I content, that in member care the *main thing* is co-laboring with Jesus Christ as his beloved, for the sake of his beloved laborers in his vineyards.

Imagine a large crane at a busy port unloading and loading shipping containers full of all manner of precious cargo, traveling to and from everywhere. What makes this kinetic and complex task possible is hidden in plain sight, the counterbalance – the heavy mass behind the crane. Without it, the crane would crash into the sea, the port along with the supply chain it supports would grind to a halt, and the crane would fundamentally fail to fulfill its purpose.

The sacredness of our calling as professionals in member care and the magnitude of the need before us, can make it all seem so impossible, especially when we forget our counterbalance. To recover the heart of member care as co-laboring with Jesus Christ as his beloved for the sake of his beloved is to lift our gaze once again with adoration and awe toward our counterbalance, our Lord Jesus Christ. To recover this, is to recover the joy it is

To recover the heart of member care as co-laboring with Jesus Christ as his beloved for the sake of his beloved is to lift our gaze once again with adoration and awe toward our counterbalance, our Lord Jesus Christ.

to be called his beloved, and the privilege to have been chosen to join him in his mission to and through his beloved laborers serving in his innumerable vineyards throughout the world.

Member Care Often Begins in Liminal Moments

The word *liminal* refers to the in-between spaces, the thresholds: it's that moment, full of promise and fear, between jumping and landing. Global workers live in liminality. They encounter all the liminal moments everyone faces as part of our human development and family life cycle, but at an intensified pace.

This liminality is further compounded by the transitions that are uniquely frequent and intense to cross-cultural ministry. For example, one couple reported that 28 units (families, couples, or singles) had joined and left their team in the 12 years they had been in the field. If you were them, would you stop investing your hearts in relationships with co-workers?

For global workers in Christ, these liminal moments inevitably crescendo. Major transitions in multiple arenas of life happen all at once. This is compounded by breakdowns in critical supportive relationships. When the go-to solutions fail, suddenly there is just

When we encounter the crescendo global workers experience, their pain can reverberate with our pain. Their despair threatens to snuff out our smoldering hope.

too much stress, too little support, and no way out. They need help. If you were in their shoes, would you wonder, as many of them do, "God, why did you call me here only to forsake me now?"

This is magnified by the ultimate liminality of the *already-not-yet* kingdom of God. In Jesus, the salvific work of the cross is complete, and the kingdom of God has come. And yet we wait .... We wait for Jesus to return and make all things well. We wait for the second coming. We wait because the kingdom of God has not yet come in glory. Where the gap between *already-not-yet* kingdom is most acute in exactly where global workers in Christ are called to live out their lives.

Consider a young family that served in a war-torn country. Their organization stopped sharing security updates out of concern that everyone would leave. When the wife gave birth to their second child, they found themselves in a state of perpetual vigilance and lost all joy. They arrived at the crescendo. While snippets of their story made it into newsletters to supporters, many other details were saved to fall as tears in the welcoming space of trusted confidants who *got it*.

Member Care Involves Uninvited Solidarity

It is here that global workers invite member care professionals to step in and help. But member care professionals also face many of the same challenges. When we encounter the crescendo global workers experience, their pain can reverberate with our pain. Their despair threatens to snuff out our smoldering hope.

This uninvited solidarity can result in vicarious trauma. As member care professionals, we may distance ourselves from those we serve as their raw pain bumps up against our unresolved pain (compassion fatigue). Or we may succumb to burnout.

Let's return to the story about the young family in a war zone. In addition to the stress of their situation, the young mom was likely experiencing postpartum depression. A member care professional, who had been in that war torn land for 15 years, told the young mom, "This is your new normal. You just have to accept it." The young couple could not *just accept it*, and so they left. But their story doesn't end there. Today, they serve refugees fleeing the war-torn country they themselves fled many years ago. That is what God's poetic grace looks like.

Jesus' Peace in the Liminality of Holy Saturday

In his passion, Jesus also experiences this crescendo of liminality. The trauma of the cross is done, and the *new day of the resurrection* has yet to dawn. The Apostles' Creed confirms what the Scriptures teach (1 Peter 3:18, 19; Ephesians 4:9, 10) that Holy Saturday is not an inconsequential dramatic pause before the grand finale. Rather, while Jesus' body rested in the tomb, his soul descended to hell to release the righteous.

Jesus enters Death – and Death encounters the author and perfecter of life! In Holy Saturday, we witness Jesus' response to liminality: a holy rest, a posture of radical acceptance, and a profound humility. It is a sacred stillness that consecrates this sabbath day. This holy sabbath rest echoes back to creation when God rested from all his labor, and it heralds the final consummation when all will repose in the reigning shalom of God's kingdom.

The pure awe of this is beautifully captured in the ancient prayers of Orthodox Christians: "In the grave bodily; in Hades with Your soul, though You were God; in Paradise with the thief;

and on the Throne with the Father and the Spirit *it is You who fills all things, O Christ the Uncircumscribable.*"[3]

This same wonder is echoed, today, in songs like "Waymaker." Its lyrics read, "Even when I can't see it, you're working. Even when I can't feel it, you're working .... Waymaker, miracle-worker, promise keeper, light in the darkness. My God, that is who you are!"[4]

We might say this Holy Saturday *work* is ontological. It is the activity of *who* Jesus is rather than *what* he does. Jesus is the Prince of Peace, and therefore his peace is powerful. With just a few words, he calms the turbulent storms around and within the disciples on the lake of Galilee (Mark 4:35–41).

With just a couple of sentences, he gives his peace to his disciples in their final meal together, saying "Peace I leave with you; my peace I give to you. I do not give to you as the world gives. Do not let your hearts be troubled, and do not let them be afraid" (John 14:27).

And Jesus does this again when he commissions his frightened disciples to join his mission after revealing himself victorious over death: "Peace be with you. As the Father has sent me, so I send you" (John 20:21). This great commission passage is especially significant for member care professionals.

Implications for Member Care Professionals

Like the disciples, we can receive Jesus' peace to go where he sends us and become instruments of his peace. When we receive this sacred stillness that Jesus Christ gives, we can simply be present and love global workers in their moments of liminality that are reaching a crescendo with his acceptance, humility, and peace. Instead of their raw pain reverberating with our unresolved

---

3 "Paschal Hours," Orthodox Prayer, accessed June 11, 2023, https://orthodoxprayer.org/Paschal%20Hours.html.

4 Sinach, "Waymaker," on *Waymaker* (Integrity Music, 2015).

With Jesus, we can enter workers' crescendo of liminality (their hell) and co-labor to bring release to these righteous ones.

pain, we can hear how parts of their story resonate with parts of our story. We can also witness how our stories are weaving into the unfolding story of the *missio Dei* – the metanarrative of God's salvific mission.

With Jesus, we can enter workers' crescendo of liminality (their hell) and co-labor to bring release to these righteous ones. We can join global workers in looking at the trauma and darkness they have endured – their Good Fridays – with authentic lament. We can join them in lifting their gaze and looking forward with expectant hope – with healing hope that the warm glow of light will dawn, life will grow, and joy will bloom once more.

Instead of uninvited, this solidarity becomes a welcomed salve of empathic communion between authentic persons. This is the pastoral ministry of every member care professional regardless of our modality of care.

Sometimes we proclaim this hope and at other times we silently steward workers' hope for them until they are ready to receive it. Regardless, as member care professionals, to co-labor with Jesus Christ, is to become men and women of peace. This prayer, attributed to St. Francis, can become our daily prayer:

Lord, make me an instrument of your peace:
where there is hatred, let me sow love;
where there is injury, pardon;
where there is doubt, faith;
where there is despair, hope;
where there is darkness, light;

where there is sadness, joy.

O divine Master, grant that I may not so much seek
to be consoled as to console,
to be understood as to understand,
to be loved as to love.

For it is in giving that we receive,
it is in pardoning that we are pardoned,
and it is in dying that we are born to eternal life.

Amen

Empowered Powerlessness through Prayer

The gap between our capacity and our awareness of the depth and breadth of need is a chasm we can't cross alone, as member care professionals. There is a freedom when we let go of unattainable expectations. This freedom from shame empowers us as professionals to uphold high ethical standards which means we consult with other member care professionals and make referrals.

We also must learn to completely depend upon a power greater than ourselves if we are really to become instruments of Jesus' peace. We must be forged into men and women of prayer who learn to see the gap and turn toward the God who creates everything from nothing.

Like the disciples who offer a boy's lunch to feed the hungry multitude, we care for global workers' well when we respond to their needs first by offering all we have in faith to Jesus. Even though it is not enough, he can bless it and make it abundantly more than enough.

We can prepare to serve global workers by inviting Jesus Christ to join us for he has promised when a few gather in his name, he will be there. As we meet, we can invite Jesus Christ to give us his heart for them and to offer his life-giving words to be "encouraging

To become men and women of prayer is to nurture the mighty faith of innocence and sincerely believe that God our Father will continue to give good gifts to his beloved.

and discerning" as Faith De La Cour says. As we depart, we can release them to Jesus's loving care and thank Jesus for working in all the concerns and longings we're now aware of. With God's help, we can become men and women who "rejoice always, pray without ceasing, give thanks in all circumstances; for this is the will of God in Christ Jesus for you" (1 Thessalonians 5:16–19).

But what does this actually look like? Let's consider this scenario. A family serving abroad is experiencing isolation. Their kids, now teenagers, are struggling but aren't asking for help. A concerned member care professional, seeking to do no harm, intervenes in prayer: "Lord, this family needs friends. I'm here now. Will you connect me with a family who can be their friends?" The prayer is miraculously answered when the member care professional meets a family from another organization who lives in their town and connects them. Years later, both families continue to serve on the field and remain close friends.

To become men and women of prayer is to nurture the mighty faith of innocence and sincerely believe that God our Father will continue to give good gifts to his beloved. We simply need to ask. To become men and women of prayer is to awaken to how God is already with us and make firm our surrendered will to God's will. To become men and women of prayer is to keep our hearts soft to the promptings of the Holy Spirit so that we can continue to co-labor with Jesus Christ in his mission to his beloved. After all, this is *his* mission, and they are his beloved. As we join him, we

There is wisdom in working out of our rest instead of resting from our work because the pilgrimage we are invited on is a lifelong interdependent journey to the kingdom of God.

become his – his men and women of peace and prayer.

Like the disciples, the challenge for those of us who are member care professionals is how quickly we misplace this sacred stillness as we seek to bring light into, but not be of, this chaotic world. Thankfully, the door of repentance is never locked. We can again, and again, and again ask for Jesus' stillness of heart and the mighty faith of innocence that we must receive if we are to join him in his mission.

We can also grow in our awareness of our nervous systems and when we are about to misplace our stillness, and in the practices and postures that nurture and protect this holy stillness where peace and prayer flourish. We can, with repentance and practice, become men and women of peace and of prayer who generously give away what we ourselves have freely received.

The Missional Promise of Holy Saturday

In the Orthodox services of Holy Saturday, the faithful listen. They listen to the Son of Man whose prophecy brings life in the valley of dry bones (Ezekiel 37:1–14). They listen to the story of Jonah tossed into the turbulent sea, swallowed by the whale to preach to the lost. They listen to the three holy youths whose steadfast faith lands them in the fiery furnace where they are joined by another (Daniel 3:1–57). They listen to Paul's exhortation that we have each been baptized into Christ's death (Romans 6:3–11). This takes on special meaning as this is the customary day of baptism for new believers.

Then they sing, crying out to the buried Lord Jesus, "Arise O God, and judge the earth, for You shall inherit all nations" (Psalm 82:8). Matthew 28:1–20 follows, and the eyes of faith witness a liturgical dialogue unfolding – finally, Jesus responds to their plea. The resurrected Lord Jesus greets the women and instructs them to send his disciples to Galilee.

The disciples go, (even though some doubt), and when they see the resurrected Lord Jesus, he speaks (to them and to us): "All authority in heaven and on earth has been given to me. Go therefore and make disciples of all nations, baptize them in the name of the Father, and of the Son, and of the Holy Spirit, and teach them to obey everything I have commanded you. And remember, I am with you always, to the end of the age" (Matthew 28:18–20).

As it turns out, Holy Saturday is not an inconsequential dramatic pause, but a liminal day full of missional promise. We have cried out to the buried Lord Jesus who has been hidden from us, to "arise and inherit all the nations." And the risen Lord Jesus reveals himself and responds: "all is mine – I have filled all things, even hell, with myself; but it is you who will go and gather my inheritance. I have given you your mission – so as you go, you needn't be afraid for I am with you and for you. Come my beloved and co-labor with me, for the sake of my beloved."

There is wisdom in working out of our rest instead of resting from our work because the pilgrimage we are invited on is a lifelong interdependent journey to the kingdom of God. Jesus who has given us this mission, leads us to our fellow pilgrims and teaches us how to co-labor with him. He gives us the Holy Spirit, and the Holy Spirit gives us the gifts and power to bear (in due season) the fruits of love, joy, peace, patience, kindness, goodness, faithfulness, gentleness, and self-control (Galatians 5:22). Along the way, we will become men and women of peace and of prayer -- it's fine if we're not there yet. One day we will become an answer to Jesus' prayer that we would be one as he and the Father are one so that our love for one another will become our witness to our lonely world that Jesus Christ has come to defeat death and save us (John 17:21).

It is in this context that we can hear Jesus' words about *the main thing* for each of us as member care professionals: "I do not call you servants any longer, because the servant does not know what the master is doing; but I have called you friends, because I have made known to you everything that I have heard from my Father. You did not choose me, but I choose you. And I appointed you to go and bear fruit, fruit that will last, so that the Father will give you whatever you ask him in my name. I am giving you these commands so that you may love one another" (John 15:15–17).

May it be so.
Amen.

GEOFF WHITEMAN, ThM, LMFT, serves member care professionals as the director of the Valeo Research Institute (valeo.global/research) and the Missio Nexus People Care and Development track co-leader. Since 2000, he has served in vocational ministry and has supported the care and training of global workers in Christ since 2007.

Questions for Reflection

- What are the practices and postures that nurture and protect the holy stillness you need personally to grow as a person of peace and prayer?
- How are these embodied in your daily and weekly habits? In the physical spaces where you live and work? In your family and community rituals and rhythms?
- What are the early signs and symptoms that you are about to misplace your stillness?
- How could you share these practices and postures with others?
- What practices and postures might your friends, families, or teams adopt for communal use?
- What might that look like here and now?
- Could sending organizations, churches, and other tertiary entities play a strategic role in nurturing and guarding this sacred stillness?
- If you are unsure about any of these questions, who is a person of peace and prayer with whom you could speak about these matters?

Additional Resources

Scan the code or visit missionexus.org/people-care for bonus resources:

The Resilient Global Worker Study. A mixed-methods, grounded theory exploration of 892 Christian Global Worker's experience and growth in resilience. https://resilientglobalworker.org.

Valeo Research Institute. Supports the development of member care professionals through solution-focused research and training. https://valeo.global/research.

Valeo Field Guide. Identified 4 outcomes for global workers in Christ who are growing in maturity and effectiveness (Equipping, Alignment, Healing, and Suffering Well). The guide can be used alone or with others to explore these outcomes and develop a personal and professional growth plan. https://valeo.global/field-guide.

Inspire Movement. Provides resources and training in missional discipleship. An idea behind the content of this chapter is that member care often responds to missed discipleship and a context for missional discipleship. https://inspiremovement.org.

E. Stanley Jones Foundation. "How to Pray Newsletter 2013." Jones' reflections on prayer are seminal to becoming persons of prayer. https://estanleyjonesfoundation.com/wp-content/uploads/2014/01/2013-How-to-Pray-Newsletter.pdf.

Further Reading

Bibliography and Additional Resources

Barton, Ruth Haley. *Embracing Rhythms of Work and Rest: From Sabbath to Sabbatical and Back Again*. InterVarsity Press, 2023.

Bremner, David. *Images of Leadership: Biblical Portraits of Godly Leaders*. Oasis International, 2021.

Brierley, Peter W. "Missionary Attrition: The ReMAP Research Report," in *Too Valuable to Lose: Exploring the Causes and Cures of Missionary Attrition*, William D. Taylor, ed. William Carey Library, 1997.

Buchanan, Mark. *The Rest of God: Restoring Your Soul by Restoring Sabbath*. Nashville, TN: Thomas Nelson Publishers, 2007.

Butterfield, Rosaria. *The Gospel Comes with a House Key: Practicing Radically Ordinary Hospitality in Our Post-Christian World* (Illinois: Crossway, 2018).

Center for Institutional Courage, https://www.institutionalcourage.org/the-call-to-courage.

Child protection, investigation, and response. https://telios.site/investigationgiveaway.

Daybreak Academy lists hospitality resources in Asia, https://daybreak-academy.org/member-care-centres-asia/.

Edmondson, Amy C. *The Fearless Organization: Creating Psychological Safety in the Workplace for Learning, Innovation, and Growth*. United Kingdom: Wiley, 2018.

Ergenbright, Dana, Stacey Conard, and Mary Crickmore. *Healing the Wounds of Trauma: How the Church Can Help (Facilitator Guide for Healing Groups)*. American Bible Society, 2021.

E. Stanley Jones Foundation. "How to Pray Newsletter 2013." Jones' reflections on prayer are seminal to becoming persons of prayer. https://estanleyjonesfoundation.com/wp-content/uploads/2014/01/2013-How-to-Pray-Newsletter.pdf.

Evangelical Council for Abuse Prevention. "Child Safety Standards." https://ecap.net/standards/.

Explicit Movement. *Brave & Beautiful*, 4-Volume Journey Book Sets. Releasing Generations, 2022. https://www.braveandbeautiful.world.

Explicit Movement. *Dream Big Journal: Keys to Unlock Your Dreams*. https://www.explicitmovement.org.

Explicit Movement. *The Birth of Explicit Movement: Discover Keys to Fulfilling Your Purpose*. https://explicitmovement.org.

Foster, Richard. *Celebration of Discipline, Special Anniversary Edition: The Path to Spiritual Growth*. San Francisco: HarperOne, 2018.

Global Member Care Network has contacts for hospitality resources around the world, https://globalmembercare.com/.

Hay, Rob, et al, eds. *Worth Keeping: Global Perspectives on Best Practice in Missionary Retention*. William Carey, 2007.

Hoke, Steve and Bill Taylor. *Global Mission Handbook: A Guide For Cross-cultural Service*. Downers Grove, IL: Intervarsity Press, 2009.

Inspire Movement. Provides resources and training in missional discipleship. An idea behind the content of this chapter is that member care often responses to missed discipleship and a context for missional discipleship. https://inspiremovement.org.

Martin-Cuellar, Ashley. "Self-Reflexivity Through Journaling: An Imperative Process for the Practicing Clinician." *The William & Mary Educational Review* 5, no. 1 (2018). https://scholarworks.wm.edu/wmer/vol5/iss1/11.

McCombs, Margi, James Covey, and Kalyn Lantz. *Healing Teens' Wounds of Trauma: How the Church Can Help*. American Bible Society.

Member Care Europe lists hospitality resources online, https://www.membercare.eu/category/resources/retreat-centres/.

Morgan, Robert J. *The Red Sea Rules: 10 God-Given Strategies for Difficult Times*. Nashville: Thomas Nelson, Inc., 2014.

Nouwen, Henri J. M. *Sabbatical Journey: The Diary of His Final Year*. New York: The Crossroad Publishing Company, 2000.

Oasis Rest International provides hosted hospitality houses for people in ministry, https://www.oasisrest.org.

O'Brien, Nancy. "Reflexivity: What Is It, and Why Is It Important in Your Community?" University of Minnesota Extension, October 4, 2021. https://extension.umn.edu/community-news-and-insights/reflexivity-what-it-and-why-it-important-your-community.

O'Connor, Mavis. "ReMAP II – Retaining Missionaries – Agency Practices: Older Sending Countries in Europe and North America."

Pohl, Christine D. *Making Room: Recovering Hospitality as a Christian Tradition* (Michigan: Wm. B. Eerdmans Publishing Co., 1999).

Rains, Hailie. "ReMAP II – Retaining Missionaries – Agency Practices: Newer Sending Countries from Africa, Asia and Latin America."

Resilient Global Workers. *The Resilient Global Worker Study*. https://resilientglobalworker.org.

Saler, Robert C. *Planning Sabbaticals: A Guide for Congregations and Their Pastors*. St. Louis, MO: Chalice Press, 2019.

Scan the QR code for bonus resources online:

Schaefer, Frauke C., and Charles A. Schaefer, eds. *Trauma and Resilience: A Handbook* Frauke C. Schaefer, MD, Inc., 2016.

Sears, Andrea D. "Missionary Attrition Survey 2017." Full results published online at https://themissionsexperience.weebly.com.

Sevier, Melissa Bane. *Journeying Toward Renewal: A Spiritual Companion for Pastoral Sabbaticals*. Bethesda, MD: Alban Institute, 2002.

Sidebotham, Theresa L. *Handling Allegations in a Ministry: Responses and Investigations*. Illumify Media, 2022.

Siegel, Daniel J. *The Developing Mind: How Relationships and the Brain Interact to Shape Who We Are*. The Guildford Press, 2020.

Simons, Sara and Jeff Simons. *Sabbaticals with Effective Recovery and Upward Momentum*. Lakewood, CO: The Way Between, Inc. https://www.thewaybetween.org/.

Simons, Sara. *Sabbatical Planning Guide (digital)*. Lakewood, CO: The Way Between, Inc, 2018. https://www.thewaybetween.org/.

Swoboda, A.J. and Matthew Sleeth. *Subversive Sabbath: The Surprising Power of Rest in a Nonstop World*. Brazos Press, 2018.

Telios Teaches. Free resources and blogs from Telios Law and Telios Teaches. https://teliosteaches.com/blog.

Telios Teaches. Protect Those in Your Care:

Telios Teaches. Purchase an annual subscription online at https://telios.site/studio.

Telios Teaches. Training from Tellios Law PLLC: Employees are happier and healthier when they are protected. See HR, Child Safety, and Professional Development training at https://teliosteaches.com/.

Thompson, Joanne. *Table Life: Savoring the Hospitality of Jesus in Your Home* (Minnesota: Beaver's Pond Press, 2011).

Valeo Field Guide. Identified 4 outcomes for global workers in Christ who are growing in maturity and effectiveness (Equipping, Alignment, Healing, and Suffering Well). The guide can be used alone or with others to explore these outcomes and develop a personal and professional growth plan. https://valeo.global/field-guide.

Valeo Research Institute. Supports the development of member care professionals through solution-focused research and training. https://valeo.global/research.

Valters Paintner, Christine. *The Artist's Rule: Nurturing Your Creative Soul with Monastic Wisdom*. Notre Dame, IN: Sorin Books, 2011.

Van der Kolk, Bessel. *The Body Keeps the Score: Brain, Mind, and Body in the Healing of Trauma*. NY: Viking Press, 2014.

Van Meter, Jim. "US Report of Findings on Missionary Retention." World Evangelical Alliance, December 2003.

Warlow, John. *The C.U.R.E. for Life: Part One; God-Centered Transformation* (Australia: Ocean Reeve Publishing, 2017).

Whiteman, Kristina. *A Treasured History: Listening to and Learning from Global Workers' Stories of Resilience*. Doctoral Dissertation, Asbury Theological Seminary, 2023. Available on ProQuest or by request from author.

Wilder, E. James. *The Pandora Problem: Facing Narcissism in Leaders and Ourselves*. United States: Deeper Walk International, 2018.

Wrobleski, Jessica. *The Limits of Hospitality* (Minnesota: Liturgical Press, 2012).

*Can you help those who need
this book to find it?*

- Share an honest review on Amazon, on social media, or through an email blast.
- Invite an author to speak on your podcast, or to your community about their chapter.
- Gift this volume to supporters to help educate them on member care and the impact their investment is making.

Scan the code below or visit missionexus.org/people-care to learn more: